Dr. Ambedkar and Nationalism

Dr. Ambedkar and Nationalism

Basant Kumar

PRABHAT
PRAKASHAN

Published by
PRABHAT PRAKASHAN PVT. LTD.
4/19 Asaf Ali Road,
New Delhi-110 002 (INDIA)
e-mail: prabhatbooks@gmail.com

ISBN 978-93-95386-75-3
DR. AMBEDKAR AND NATIONALISM
by Shri Basant Kumar

Edition
2026

Price
₹ 500.00 (Rupees Five Hundred only)

Printed at
R-Tech Offset Printers, Delhi

Dedicated to my revered father and
eminent trade union leader
Shri Guru Prasad
who fought for the rights of labourers and
the working class
inculcating in me high values.

'We are Indians first and last and
as per the time and circumstances,
nothing under the sun shall stop
the country from becoming a super power.'

—Dr. B.R. Ambedkar

सत्यमेव जयते

अध्यक्ष, लोक सभा

SPEAKER, LOK SABHA

Message

I am happy to learn that a book, titled *Dr. Ambedkar and Nationalism*, the architect of the Constitution of India and the recipient of Bharat Ratna, has been written by Basant Kumar and is being published by Prabhat Prakashan.

Babasaheb Bhimrao Ambedkar devoted his entire life to fighting against inequality and fighting for the rights of the downtrodden and the oppressed. The country is indebted to him for his untiring efforts to bring about a new social order and for his contribution to the framing of the Constitution of India.

It is inevitable that social and political changes will continue to happen in our society like in any other society, but the concept of equality promoted by Dr. Ambedkar is no less relevant today. We have been able to develop as a nation because we have always been inspirational in the implementation of our development activities and policies and have shown the way to establish an egalitarian society.

I congratulate the popular and learned author Basant Kumar for writing this interesting book. The publication of this book on Dr. Ambedkar is another attempt to throw light on the life and works of this great leader and to express his gratitude towards him. I wish them success in all their future endeavours.

(Om Birla)

Yogi Adityanath

Number: G 204/CM-2/2020
Lok Bhawan
Lucknow-226001

Date : ....

Chief Minister
Uttar Pradesh

Message

I am pleased to know that a book titled *Dr. Ambedkar and Nationalism*, written by Basant Kumar is being published by Prabhat Prakashan, on the life of Dr. Bhimrao Ambedkar, the architect of the Constitution of India and the recipient of Bharat Ratna.

Babasaheb Dr. Bhimrao Ambedkar played a vital role in uniting the people, belonging to the last rung of the society, poors and the downtrodden, to bring in mainstream of society and nation. Dr. Ambedkar made many provisions in the Constitution of India to provide social justice to the deprived and marginalised sections. The publication of this book in the memory of such a great man is highly commendable. I believe that essential information regarding the inspirational personality of Babasaheb Dr. Ambedkar will be incorporated into the book.

My heartiest congratulations on the successful and purposeful publication of the book.

(Yogi Adityanath)
Chief Minister
Uttar Pradesh

BRS
Charitable Trust

Bhagvanti Devi-Raj Murti Saroj (BRS)
Charitable Trust
Mohariyawan, Machhali Shahar, Jaunpur (UP)

Message

It gives me great pleasure to congratulate Shri Basant Kumar on publication of the book *'Dr. Ambedkar and Nationalism'*. Despite large amount of published literature on the life and work of Bharat Ratna Dr. B.R. Ambedkar, this book provides a unique insight into Dr. Ambedkar's contribution and thoughts on Indian politics, economic development, and social empowerment.

Dr. Ambedkar's contribution on provisions for positive discrimination (reservation) in Indian constitution is one of most common topics in books available around us. This book provides much deeper analysis of Dr. Ambedkar's contribution to modern India. Dr. Ambedkar was the first Indian to receive doctorate in economics abroad. He received two doctorate degrees in the field of economics from two prestigious universities: Columbia University (USA) and London School of Economics, University of London (UK). The details of Dr. Ambedkar's thoughts and opinion analysed in this book convey the relevance in understanding political and socio-economic issues of modern India.

This book illustrates how the Indian youth can learn and benefit from Dr. Ambedkar's analysis of Indian geopolitics and socio-economics in the context of modern India.

(Dr. Devendra Prakash Saroj)
B-Tech, M-Tech (IIT) PhD (Italy) CEnv FHEA (UK)
Head of Centre for Environmental Health and Engineering
University of Surrey, United Kingdom

Secretary General
Bhagvanti Devi-Raj Murti Saroj (BRS) Charitable Trust

Foreword

Indian culture is established on the concept of *vasudaiva kutumbakam*. Our cultural spread can be profoundly felt only in this notion of considering the whole world as a family, beyond the boundaries of a particular region. There is a prayer in *Yajurveda*—

'वयम राष्ट्रे जाग्रयाम पुरोहिताः'

'Vayam raashtre jaagrayam purohitaah'

We should awaken the nation by becoming pioneer priests. This Indian culture is the basis of nationalism. The State or any particular ideology has no place here. Provincial, regional and ethnicity have never been accepted at any level in Indian culture and that is why nationalism means the mindset of thinking above all religions and castes. There is a desire to live life not only for oneself, but also for others. Indian culture witnesses the abode of God in a tree as well; feels the presence of a mother in the river. Tulsidas has said, '*Siyaram may sab jag jani.*'

Maharishi Ved Vyas has written in the epic *Mahabharata*, '*Yanna Bharate tann Bharate*'. That is, the one who is not in India is nowhere and the one, who is in India, is everywhere. This is the basis of nationalism. The entirety of our culture can be felt in it. So I believe that 'nationalism' is not just a word; it is a meaningful Indian cultural dialogue. The proclamation of

'*Vande Mataram*', the sublime vision of Swami Vivekananda, the brilliant thoughts of Madhav Sadashivrao Golwalkar and the Integral Humanism of Pt. Deendayal Upadhyay, etc. retain the light of nationalism in a way.

If there has been any strong advocate of nationalism in India, it has been Madhav Sadashivrao Golwalkar 'Guruji', the second Sarsanghachalak of Rashtriya Swayamsevak Sangh. He has written: 'Our idea of a Hindu *rashtra* is not just a bundle of political and economic rights; it is cultural in essence. Its life has been created out of our ancient and sublime life values and only the fervent cultivation of the spirit of our culture can provide us with the right vision of our national life. By innovation of our culture we mean to bring back to life those eternal life ideals, which nurtured our nation's life for thousands of years and gave immortality.'

The path of socio-economic upliftment of Scheduled Castes in independent India was opened due to this thinking of Guruji's lofty ideas of nationalism. Nationalism means that all the citizens of the country, irrespective of their sect, caste, language or region, are committed to the nation by rising above the boundaries. There is no place for personal ideology and selfishness there. In this regard, I am especially remembering the words of Pt. Vidyanivas Mishra, who said, 'If the sect is confined to self-defence, it leads to inertia.' That's the truth. There is no place for communalism and casteism in a democracy. The nation is sapped by casteism. The relaxation of caste sentiment at the social level and the predominance in the political field is a situation of contradictions. I do not consider this to be correct. The slogan of the *bhakti* movement was, '*Jaati paati na pooche koye, Hari ko bhaje so Hari ka hoye*'.

The framers of the constitution knew that the caste system and democracy could not co-exist, so they made such rules in the constitution by which there would be no discrimination against any citizen of the country. Equality should be maintained at all levels. The nation is formed by its traditions, culture, religion, castes and languages put together, so there is no place for narrow-mindedness in nationalism.

The Indian Constitution gives equal rights to every citizen of the country. In the last meeting of the Constituent Assembly, Babasaheb Ambedkar, an outstanding scholar, spoke of social democracy. In the Constituent Assembly, the main task of proving the provisions of the draft and their justification rested on him and on the members of the drafting committee. In the draft of the constitution that he made with his able colleagues, he gave a voice to the country's traditions, faith and beliefs. In the statements by Dr. Ambedkar in the Constituent Assembly, there is a unique amalgamation of politics, law, history and philosophy. There is a sense of equality for all and not just for any one caste. In November 1948, while presenting his proposal to consider the draft of the constitution, he said, 'We have called India not a union of states, but a Union State.' I agree Dr. Ambedkar was concerned about the social divisions in India, which is why he said that if we want to construct democracy, then we have to recognise the obstacles in our path because the grand palace of the constitution can stand only on the foundation of loyalty of the people in a democracy.

Dr. Ambedkar's thoughts are actually related to that nationalism in which there is no distinction of caste, *varna*, class or religion between individuals. Every citizen of the country is basically equal. There is harmony in all of us under the social system and social thinking. That is why our nation is an excellent example of unity in diversity.

The Preamble of the Indian Constitution talks of equality and fraternity for all citizens. On the basis of what Dr. Babasaheb Ambedkar had said in his last speech of the Constituent Assembly, while mentioning the anomalies of social life, many amendments were made to the constitution with respect to that and whose role was only to establish social, economic and political harmony.

As the architect of the Indian Constitution, Dr. Ambedkar took three words from the French Revolution – Liberty, Equality and Fraternity. These words, included in the core of the constitution, had deeply influenced his political and social life and philosophy. Therefore, the right to equality has been explained through Articles 14 to 18 in the Fundamental Rights of the Constitution. In this regard, the right to freedom has been given through Articles 19 to 22 of the Constitution and the right against exploitation has been granted to citizens in Articles 23 and 24. The right to freedom of religion has been provided in the Indian Constitution through Articles 25 to 28. I believe that the Constitution of India is one of the constitutions around the world, in which the Fundamental Rights have been elaborately explained.

I have studied Dr. Ambedkar's ideas continuously from time to time and on that basis, I am of the opinion that his nationalism was not bound by narrow-mindedness, which is why many times it is sad to read that he is seen only as a leader of a particular caste or class, under narrow thinking. I think it goes against his grand personality. He should not be looked at with a narrow perspective. In the role he has played in nation-building, there has been the lofty idea of seeing everyone as equal. It also needs to be understood that Article 370 was added to the Constitution against his will, which was removed after 72 years of Independence by the strong will and determination of the current Prime Minister Shri Narendra Modi and Home Minister Shri Amit Shah.

The idea of a Uniform Civil Code of Conduct was in line with Dr. Ambedkar's basic concept of equality and the creation of which had started even before Independence, and the plan to pass it was initiated by Dr. Ambedkar through Dr. Syama Prasad Mookerji. If we go into the totality of Dr. Ambedkar's thoughts, then it will also appear that the seeds of equality are there with the unity and integrity of the country. Today the country is progressing continuously under the leadership of Prime Minister Narendra Modi due to his magnificent vision of treating everyone as equal in the country under cultural nationalism. The Government of India's Pt. Deendayal Grameen Kaushal Yojana is a reflection of Babasaheb's ideals. The basic objective of this scheme for skill development in rural and backward areas is that everyone can progress equally. Prime Minister Modi has taken forward Babasaheb's vision of gender equality by delivering the right to adoption and the right to property. Inspired by his economic vision, the Pradhan Mantri Jan-Dhan Scheme was started in the country. The aim is that the country can develop continuously with the thinking of equality.

I consider this book *Dr. Ambedkar and Nationalism* important as it is an extension of his noble vision. It is rightly said by Prime Minister Narendra Modi in this book that Dr. Ambedkar's message of equality and justice is relevant even today. His economic thought was '*Bahujan hitay bahujan sukhay*'.

The scholarly author Shri Basant Kumar has given great thought to the glorious thinking of Dr. Ambedkar in this book. He has also given a detailed discussion of Dr. Ambedkar's thoughts regarding the power participation of the deprived society, women's empowerment, integral humanism and Dalits adopting Islam and other religions in today's context of the Civil Amendment Act. The entire book gives a new vision to understand Dr. Ambedkar in totality. This is an important work of his life and philosophy. For this, I congratulate and convey my best wishes to the author Shri Basant Kumar.

—Kalraj Mishra

Preface

Bharat Ratna Babasaheb Dr. Bhimrao Ramji Ambedkar is like that comet of Indian politics that will continue to shine in the world's politics and not only in India but in the entire world, till eternity. The entire society and the country will remain indebted to him for the contribution he has made as the country's constitution-maker, a social reformer, an economist and a follower of Buddhism in the last years of his life. Some Leftists and people who call themselves Ambedkarites try to forcefully present him as a Dalit icon, which is totally unjust. Dr. Ambedkar was a nationalist in the real sense – he came to India despite receiving higher education abroad and started his struggle for the service of Bharat, but unfortunately the Congress, which was ruling the country, did not give Babasaheb the respect he deserved. His oil painting in the Central Hall of Parliament was put up 42 years after Independence in 1989 by the government of late Prime Minister Vishwanath Pratap Singh and on the advice of late Atal Bihari Vajpayee and Lal Krishna Advani, he was given the 'Bharat Ratna' posthumously. When Dr. Ambedkar contested the Lok Sabha elections, the Congress, which became benevolent to Dalits, opposed him because the Congress did not want Dr. Ambedkar to win the election and enter the Lok Sabha; now the same Congress says that the Sangh and Ambedkar are anti-Dalit. His election campaign was conducted by his election agent Dattopant Thengadi, who was a member of the RSS and was a propounder of equality and played an important role in the field of labour welfare.

Dr. Ambedkar is the architect of the constitution of this country and played an important role as the chairman of the drafting committee. Despite facing innumerable neglects, reproaches and insults in his life, he did not allow even the slightest sound of a hurt mind to enter while making the constitution, nor did he ever say that he was not encouraged to obtain higher education abroad. Despite this, he said that he would stay in India and play an important role in making India a strong nation.

What a daunting task he faced in the making of the constitution and this can be gauged from the fact that nearly 7,435 proposals were made during the constitution-making and out of which, more than 4,100 proposals were set aside. Later 2,431 proposals were successful in getting approval. For the dignified life of every citizen of India, Dr. Ambedkar gave a system of fundamental rights in the Indian Constitution, under which the right to equality through Articles 14, 15, 16, 17, and 18, the right to freedom in Articles 19, 20, 21, 22 while Articles 23 and 24 granted the right to fight exploitation. Babasaheb knew very well that India is a country of different religions and religious beliefs. For this reason, the right to religious freedom was given in Articles 25, 26, 27, and 28 in order to protect these fundamental rights; Article 32 was provided under which any person could directly approach the Supreme Court and file a petition if the fundamental rights were violated. Under Articles 29 and 30, minorities were given the right to establish their own educational institutions on their own under their social and educational rights.

Babasaheb's contribution as an economist and a visionary

is significant. Many laws were made for the welfare of workers and for the protection of labour rights. It made arrangements for providing minimum wages to workers, a provident fund for the workers and stressed on better communication between the workers and the employers. He created the constitution of the country as well as an economic structure. The plan to set up the Central Waterways Irrigation and Navigation Commission and Damodar Valley Project, Hirakud Dam Project and several projects related to water were brain-child of Babasaheb. At the time of the establishment of the Reserve Bank of India, Hilton Young Commission had made use of the suggestions made by Dr. Ambedkar in his research at Columbia University, he wrote a thesis 'National Dividend of India', which was published in 1924, in which he gave the concept of the Finance Commission and based on that concept, the Finance Commission was established in India. Even 70 years ago, he talked about women's empowerment and giving equal rights to both men and women because he was deeply influenced by Savitribai Phule. He gave protection to women by giving them the right to adoption and right to property.

He was a strong advocate of unity and harmony in the country, that is why when Sheikh Abdullah asked Pt. Jawaharlal Nehru for a special status for Kashmir by adding Article 370 to the Constitution, Pt. Nehru sent Sheikh Abdullah to Dr. Ambedkar, the chairman of the drafting committee. But Dr. Ambedkar refused it because he was a strong opponent of Article 370. It was due to Nehru's insistence that Article 370 came into force on the basis of majority, but Dr. Ambedkar stipulated in the constitution that this article was temporary. And this divisive provision was finally abolished in August 2019 through the bold decision taken by Prime Minister Shri Narendra Modi.

After becoming Prime Minister and to give concrete shape to the economic vision of Dr. Ambedkar, Prime Minister Narendra Modi set the basic *mantra* of his administration '*Sabka Saath, Sabka Vikas*'. Modi launched the *'Jan-Dhan Yojana'* through which crores of people in the country joined the banking system by opening accounts in banks. A special session was organised in the Parliament to celebrate the 125th birth anniversary of Dr. Ambedkar, whose role we cannot deny in maintaining the integrity of the country. Speaking in the Parliament, Prime Minister Modi said that all Babasaheb did for preserving the dignity of the marginalised and oppressed people and in the making of the Constitution should serve as a guide for us. To pass this glory to our future generations and to make them aware of it, it is necessary to strengthen the democracy of our country. If Dr. Ambedkar had not played such an important role in chalking out the constitution, then perhaps our constitution would have missed becoming a social document. This social document was made because the pain and sufferings that Babasaheb endured emerged in the form of words which created this great document, the Constitution of India. It was Babasaheb's greatness that he suffered various tortures throughout his life but he did not let it come out in the form of revenge anywhere during the constitution-making. In the constitution, he tried to integrate everyone and described in his speech on 25 November, 1949 how the citizens of independent India should behave to maintain the democratic order. 'If we wish to maintain democracy not merely in form, but also in fact, what must we do? The first thing, in my judgement, what we must do is to hold fast to constitutional methods of achieving our social and economic objectives... Where constitutional methods are open, there can be no justification for unconstitutional methods. These methods are nothing but the grammar of anarchy, and the sooner they are abandoned, the better for us.'

Speaking on the special occasion of Dr. Ambedkar's 125 birth anniversary in the Parliament, the then Home Minister Shri Rajnath Singh said, 'Many people try to present Babasaheb Bhimrao Ambedkar in common parlance as a Dalit leader, but in my view, he should not be seen from this narrow perspective. The kind of role he has played to maintain the unity of India, Babasaheb Ambedkar is indeed a national sage (Rajarshi).'

As a nationalist, the whole country is indebted to Babasaheb Dr. Bhimrao Ambedkar for making India a strong and united nation. Through this book, an attempt has been made to make his efforts and achievements accessible to the people and remove the illusion that he strove only for the welfare of the downtrodden. He remained determined to work for the welfare and development of all the Dalits, minorities, women and youth. I would like to express my gratitude to all my colleagues for their invaluable cooperation in this creation.

I cannot forget the valuable suggestions given by Dr. Krishna Gopal, Sarkaryavah of RSS and my friend Shri Vinod Kumar Sonkar, Member Parliament to include the speech of Prime Minister Narendra Modi delivered at the special session of Parliament on the eve of the 125th anniversary of Babasaheb and views of other dignitaries like Shri Lal Krishna Advani and Dr. Murli Manohar Joshi. Lastly, I would like to mention the strenuous effort put in by Harshita Verma, a law student, in making successful this version of the book.

—Basant Kumar

Contents

From the Pen of the Author

Babasaheb Ambedkar: A Visionary

—Narendra Modi

The manner in which the respected Speaker presented the importance of the constitution, the usefulness of the constitution and the far-sightedness of the great man of the nation behind the making of the constitution is important in the history of Parliament. I congratulate the Parliament for highlighting the importance of the constitution and commitment to it through discussions and by displaying interest in this matter.

Our constitution possesses the power to bind our country which is home to all kinds of diversities. Therefore, the need of the hour is to convey the sanctity of the constitution, the power of the constitution and the information contained in the constitution to the people. The country is celebrating the 125th birth anniversary of Babasaheb Ambedkar for which this programme was organised by linking it with the Parliament. Subsequently it will be taken to public meetings. There should be such a system in the schools too so that discussion on the constitution is widespread. This country has progressed

* On the eve of Constitution day, excerpts taken from speech of Prime Minister in Parliament on 27th November, 2015.

through austerities observed by the people. Everyone has had a role to play in the constitution and we have a perfect constitution, which embodies dignity and unity for India.

We cannot deny the role of Babasaheb in preserving the dignity of the common man and the integrity of the country. This country has been built through the tenacity and sacrifice of many great men who hold their own importance. Today, this programme on the constitution has not been conceived for the first time. After 60 years of adoption of the constitution, in the year 2009, when I was the Chief Minister of Gujarat, we had taken out a procession on behalf of the state government by beautifying the Constitution of India and carrying it on an elephant's back through the streets. As the Chief Minister, I had walked in front of the elephant to convey to the people the importance of the constitution. This way we celebrated 60 years of the constitution on the soil of Gujarat. In a country so diverse, what an appreciable work Ambedkar and his associates must have done in drafting the constitution within three years. This may not have been difficult for many other countries but in a country with 12 religions, 122 languages, more than 1,800 dialects and different systems of worship, it was no mean task that the framers of our constitution performed. The stipulations in the constitution serve as our guide today. We have to pass this glory to the generations to come. To strengthen democracy in India, it becomes our responsibility to convey the spirit of the constitution and the power that the constitution bestows upon the people.

If one wants to attack the government, Babasaheb provides the answer and if someone has to defend himself, then also Babasaheb conveys the reply. This depicts what a great visionary he was that even today the constitution serves as a guide for those who protest, for those who run the government and for those who are neutral. It has been a speciality of Babasaheb that his thoughts prove beneficial for every period, for every generation and for every section. There was a strength in his thoughts which showed his dedication to the nation and his far-sightedness in viewing what the country would be like after 100 years. When I look at this constitution, I find this is a document that has sections on what we should do and not do, what path to adopt and how to run the government and Parliament. Granville Austin had remarked about the Constitution of India, "It is first and foremost a social document... otherwise the constitution is expected to be a legal document." Had it not been for Dr. Ambedkar, then perhaps our constitution could not have served better the country and its governance. This social document was prepared through Babasaheb Ambedkar's pain, suffering and the torture that he underwent during his childhood and the extract of his sufferings were turned into words by him. As a son of a Dalit mother, he suffered torture, humiliation and neglect from birth till death. When given the responsibility of drafting the constitution, there was the possibility of that bitterness and poison surfacing somewhere in the constitution, but it was Babasaheb's greatness that despite his sufferings, he did not allow any sense of revenge to creep anywhere in the constitution. How strong must have been the inner thinking of this great man who drank all the poison and left nectar for us. In our constitution, there is an effort to integrate everyone, to include each of us and keep our welfare at heart. Is it any wonder that whenever we think or see or read the Constitution of India, our heads bow down in reverence to this great stalwart of India.

On 25th November, 1949, Babasaheb Ambedkar spoke on how citizens should behave in maintaining freedom and the democratic order in free India, "What should we do if we want to maintain democracy not only in its form, but in reality? The first thing that we should do, in my view, is to firmly adhere to constitutional methods to achieve our social and economic goals. Where constitutional methods are open, there cannot be justification for any unconstitutional methods, which are nothing but seeds for spreading anarchy."

As the chairman of the Drafting Committee, Dr. Babasaheb Ambedkar said about Article 368: "The Constitution is the basic document, which defines the position and powers of the three organs of the State – the executive, the judiciary and the legislature. It also defines the powers of the executive and the powers of the legislature toward the citizens, as in the case of our Fundamental Rights. In fact, the purpose of the constitution is not only to create organs of the State, but to limit its authority, because if no limit is imposed on the authority of the organ, then it will lead to complete autocracy. If the legislature is free to make any law, the executive is free to make any decision, then the Supreme Court is free to interpret the law."

On implementation of the constitution, Babasaheb said, "I feel that no matter how good the Constitution is, but those who are called upon to implement it may be an ineligible group; however, no matter how bad a constitution is, it can prove to be good if the group implementing it is good. Therefore, preserving the sanctity of the constitution is the responsibility of all of us. Compromise should rule, but all things fail when the matter is weighed on the scales of minority and majority."

I still remember it was the government of Atal Bihari Vajpayee in power when the test of the majority was being held. When the government of Atalji fell by one vote with Girdhar Gomango, who had become the Chief Minister of Odisha, voting against Vajpayee in the Lok Sabha. Whether the constitution is in good or bad hands, there cannot be a better example than this. Atalji's speech on that day and the height from which he left the government cannot be forgotten. Our society is thousands of years old and there are many evils in it, but several great men have come to remove those evils. When there was a ruthless system against Dalits, the oppressed, exploited, deprived, and poor in the society, then Jyotiba Phule and Babasaheb Ambedkar arrived on the field to fight for them, and great men like Narsi Mehta and Mahatma Gandhi took up the cause of removal of untouchability, when corruption was at its peak. In other words, whenever evil entered the society, some great person arose to fight that evil in every period.

Once, in the Parliament, socialist leader Dr. Ram Manohar Lohia told Pandit Nehru through statistics that his policies were wrong. At this, Pandit Nehru stood up and replied, "I cannot deny your statistics." This was the height of our constitution and values. Today we have the constitution based on the thinking of these great men and which no one can wipe away in today's times. If Babasaheb Ambedkar had not stipulated reservation in the constitution, then what would have been the condition of Dalits, the oppressed and the exploited sections of the society? God has given the Dalits all the desirable physical and mental attributes like any other strata of society but due to lack of opportunities and the prevailing caste system, they faced all kinds of humiliation and harassment at every step. It is the responsibility of us all to provide opportunities because an egalitarian society can be established only when all classes of people are empowered. Be it, men or women, no matter to which caste or creed they belong, or which language they speak, or which part of the country they live in, all should be empowered.

What can be a greater privilege in a country that has 800 million youth who are able-bodied working hands required for building and boosting a democracy? Babasaheb did a great job by fixing the limit of eight hours for the workers. Earlier, when a worker wanted money, there was no source from which he could withdraw the money. Today the Employee's Provident Fund (EPF) account travels from one place to another and the worker can withdraw any amount from his fund. Theirony was that unclaimed Rs 27,000 crore lay with the government. So a Universal Account Number (UAN) was fixed and now the situation is such that wherever the worker goes, his UAN number moves with him.

The next step is to increase the minimum pension to Rs 1,000 and the Direct Benefit Scheme should be linked with the Aadhaar card. The Bonus Act for the workers is to be introduced in Parliament under which there is provision for increasing the amount from 3,500 to 7,000 rupees and the Cabinet has passed the qualification limit from 10,000 to 21,000.

I want to reiterate that the government has only one religion – 'India First'; and the government has only one scripture – the Constitution of India. The country should be run according to the constitution because then only can the country derive its strength from the strength of the constitution. There is no reason for any doubt or apprehension in it.

□

Immortal Light for the Society under Cloud

—Narendra Modi

Babasaheb Ambedkar's message of equality and justice for all is as relevant today as it was when it was stipulated in the constitution of the country. The state government of Maharashtra had Occupied a bungalow located at 10 King Henry Road in northwest London and covering an area of 2,050 square feet, purchased in August 2015 for approximately £4 million. Ambedkar used to live in this building in the 1920s as a student during the British era and India acquired this bungalow only two months ago.

Babasaheb's contribution to the uplift of the downtrodden and backward classes is invaluable. I am very excited about this UK trip. Be it a Dalit, oppressed, exploited, deprived, or backward, for any Indian who faces difficulties, this building of Babasaheb Ambedkar inspires that if the will is strong, one can overcome all kinds of adversities and move forward in life. It will be found that this is the same place where Babasaheb Ambedkar had done penance. Today, the Government of India and the state governments give scholarships to promising Dalits, tribals and backward classes of the society for studying

* Lecture on the occasion of inauguration of memorial in the memory of Dr. Ambedkar in London on 14th November, 2015.

abroad. I am sure when our children go abroad, this place where Babasaheb Ambedkar lived will become a centre of pilgrimage and inspiration for them. The memorial also houses the pedestal used by Babasaheb.

Babasaheb was a leader belonging to a unique category as he devoted his entire life to the welfare of the nation. Nearly 80 per cent of India's Dalits were socially and financially deprived; on seeing their plight, Babasaheb resolved to free them from that curse. He was a social reformer, politician, economist, lawyer, writer, thinker, philosopher, minister and constitution-maker. His multifaceted personality brought glory to India as his name spread all over the world. Ambedkar was an immortal light in the darkened social humanity. Whatever he contemplated, he said and worked towards fulfilling the same. He had the courage to talk and behave accordingly. His integrity and tenacity made him extraordinary. He was not a mere idealistic dreamer; his ideal conduct showed the path to the society.

Considering human life as indivisible, he emphasised its totality and did not leave any aspect of life incomplete. As in charge of justice, Ambedkar became the representative of the society by adopting the basic principle of Dalit welfare and creating awareness among them. The truth is that he had no craving for position, power or fame; he considered it as his duty to work for the welfare of society. He taught mankind to live and rise above narrow thinking. Life is lived by all, but in reality, he was the one who lived it best, who thought the most, felt the deepest and acted the best. Human life is not evaluated on the basis of longevity, health, or mere wealth accumulation or power, but on the basis of those qualities and deeds, by which a person contributes to social uplift and progress. He did many favours to this country by rising above honour and humiliation, victory and defeat – due to which the entire country is indebted to him.

□

Babasaheb's Economic Thought: *'Bahujan Hitaya Bahujan Sukhai'*

—Narendra Modi

On 6th December, 2015, Prime Minister Narendra Modi released two commemorative coins in the name of Dr. Ambedkar and said, 'There are very few people who live up to 60 years in some form or the other. Dr. Ambedkar is one among them. The more we remember his thoughts, the more we respect his vision of the whole of mankind. He was a visionary and a deep thinker." Everyone knows about Babasaheb's contribution to social justice, but his economic thoughts were not discussed in depth. Be it the Finance Commission or the Reserve Bank of India, it was all a result of his imagination. Dr. Ambedkar's views on subjects like women empowerment, the federal structure of India, finance and education were commendable. When we look at Babasaheb in the context of today's problems, we can see how far-sighted a person he was, how deeply he could think and how much inclusive imagination he possessed. Discussion took place in both the houses of Parliament on the occasion of his 125th birth anniversary. The members tried to understand and relate with

---

* Speech on 6th December, 2015, on the occasion of the issuance of coins in memory of Dr. Babasaheb Ambedkar

Babasaheb's point of view. Questions also arose in the minds of some people that we know what is 15th August, what is 26th January, but from where did Modiji bring 26th November? If they had read Dr. Ambedkar, they probably would not have asked such a question.

Look at Ambedkar's diversity – he suffered at the hands of the society, he was unhappy with society and there was resentment in his mind towards the society, so he harboured a strong desire to bring a change in the society. Yet, when he stayed outside India for five years, he wrote: 'What is untouchability here, I have forgotten. There is respect all around here, instead of the humiliating state; yet, I will go back there.'

Look at his second characteristic when, in spite of being a victim of resentment, pain and suffering in society, his devotion towards India never waned. He was always proud of the cultural heritage of India. When working on his thesis for doing Ph.D., his choice of the subject was Ancient Indian Commerce, which is proof that he had an unwavering faith in the dignity of India. The second aspect, I believe is that the policymakers of today, in the context of global economy, think in coordination with Babasaheb's economic thinking. In other words, it is going to take time for the world to reach Babasaheb's vision. As far as India is concerned, his economic thought on this subject was very simple – '*Bahujan hitay, bahujan sukhai*'.

Today we talk about the Reserve Bank, but when the country was not Independent, Babasaheb in his thesis had envisioned the establishment of Reserve Bank in India. When we talk about our federal structure, we talk about the Finance Commission, what will the State get and how much will it get. But before Independence of the country, Babasaheb had put forward the concept of a Finance Commission and how should the property be divided between the states and the Centre. In the light of his thoughts, RBI and institutions like the Finance Commission are today in existence. We are talking of the interlinking of rivers and strangely enough, just two days ago when I was having a meal with the Chief Justice of India, he asked me as to what was happening about constructing the river grid. Dr. Ambedkar had envisioned the creation of a water commission in that era. Is it not surprising that a visionary like him could think so far ahead?

Babasaheb highlighted the importance of women in development and contribution to the country. At that time, the Dalits, the women and the oppressed were being humiliated. It was on seeing their plight that this great man conceived of equal partnership between man and woman during their development journey. His insistence on teaching and learning imparted new strength to the society.

I wish to discuss Babasaheb Ambedkar who was the life of India. In his last few days, his physical condition deteriorated to such an extent that his body became home to several diseases. During his childhood and youth, he could not find the opportunities or even the food to build his body, while during his last days on earth, when there were some possibilities in life, he had expended himself on serving the society and the country. Whatever work he would undertake, he would put his soul into it; that is, he would get completely immersed in the task on hand it and so a situation came when his body had reached its final limit, he could not do all that he had wanted to do. He was busy writing his book even four days before his death. His first book was his thesis 'Indian Ancient Commerce' and his last book was *Buddha and Karl Marx*. At that time, Karl Marx's thinking was quite popular all over the world including in India, and so he wrote *Buddha and Karl Marx*, based on the thoughts of Gautam Buddha and urged for establishing an all-inclusive '*bahujan hitaya, bahujan sukhai*'.

If one thinks of his economic thought, then one finds that it is relevant to the soil of India, where Buddha had played a significant role. It was Dr. Ambedkar, the sage, the force, that gifted us a vast social outlook in a legal perspective and laid the foundation stone for the basic modes of running a society and nation. Today we have to remember the great man with such great pride that it prompted the Government of India to issue coins in his memory. Though many coins have been issued, but for every Dalit or oppressed in the society, holding Rs 125 in his pocket is bound to bring happiness and pride. I am satisfied to have fulfilled this responsibility!

□

Government's Commitment to Babasaheb's Mission

—Narendra Modi

This Centre will help in taking Babasaheb's teachings and vision to the people. The Dr. Ambedkar International Centre for Socio-Economic Transformation has been built within the Dr. Ambedkar International Centre. This Centre will become important for conducting research on social and economic subjects. Strange as may seem, even after years of his departure, attempts were made to erase his contribution to nation-building, but these people could not remove Babasaheb's lofty ideals from people's memory. It is no wonder that influenced by Babasaheb's life and contribution many are following the path shown by him. We are all indebted to Babasaheb for his contribution to nation-building. It is the endeavor of our government that his ideas should reach as many people as possible, especially the young generation who should know about him and study his vision.

In this government, important places related to Babasaheb's life are being developed as pilgrimage sites. A national memorial is being constructed at the house where

* Speech of Prime Minister Narendra Modi on 7th December, 2017, on the eve of inauguration of Ambedkar International Study Centre.

Babasaheb died – Alipur in Delhi. Similarly, the Ambedkar Memorial is being constructed on the land taken from Indu Mills in Mumbai. The Diksha Bhoomi in Nagpur is also being developed further. This *panchteerth* is in a way a tribute to Babasaheb from today's generation. Similarly, Mahu, where Babasaheb was born, is also being developed as a place of pilgrimage. The Maharashtra government is developing the London house, where Babasaheb lived, to convert it into a memorial.

Last year a sixth shrine was devoted to him in a virtual world as Bharat Interface for Money, i.e. Bhim APP is a tribute to Babasaheb's economic vision by this government. Bhim APP has come as a boon for the poor Dalits, backwards, exploited, downtrodden persons, who have faced the social evils prevalent in the country throughout their life. We have to accept that even after so many years, we have not been able to fulfil the expectations of Babasaheb.

The caste acquired at the time of birth by some people becomes more important than the land acquired at the time of birth. Today's generation has the capacity to eliminate these social evils. I will give full credit to the new generation for the change we are seeing since the last 15-20 years.

Even after years of Independence, a situation prevails in our country where there is no equality among millions of people. The very basic amenities, like electricity, water, a small house and life insurance remain huge challenges for them. In the last three-and-a-half years, we have tried to fulfil Babasaheb's dream of building a social democracy. The plans of this government have been to strengthen social democracy. Those who have not gone to the village for a long time, can now see how the scheme called the Ujjwala Yojana has bridged this gap. Earlier only some houses had gas connections while the others used to burn wood or cow dung cakes. This was the biggest example of social discrimination which this government has abolished.

Swachh Bharat Mission has brought a sense of equality among the women of the village. It was an anomaly in the village with only a few houses provided with toilets while the rest used to go to the fields to relieve themselves. Gradually toilets are being built in most houses. Earlier the coverage was 40 per cent but now it has increased to more than 70 per cent. At the core of Babasaheb's ideology lay the following principles – equality of honour, equality of law, equality of rights, equality of human dignity and equality of opportunity, many of which are being implemented now.

Babasaheb had hoped that the successive governments in India would run without making any distinction of creed or class or caste. Today, in every scheme of this government, an attempt is being made to grant equal rights to all without any discrimination. The delay in any of the schemes is considered criminal negligence by this government. Take the case of the Ambedkar International Centre whichwas supposed to have been built in the year 1992, but nothing happened for 23 years. The foundation stone was laid by the government in power while the inauguration is being done by this government. The pace at which this Centre was completed before its scheduled date, in the same manner, work is being done on many schemes so as to implement them before the scheduled date. Once all the arrangements are in place, we shall further reduce the time frame so that the target can be achieved swiftly.

The time limit for 'Mission Indradhanush' has been reduced by two years. Under this scheme, more than 25 crore children and more than 70 lakh women have been vaccinated so far. Earlier the government's target was to achieve full immunisation cover in the country by 2020. This has now been reduced to 2018. You will be surprised to know that about 60 per cent of the beneficiaries of Mudra Yojana, which changes the meaning of employment in the country, are Dalits, backwards and tribals. So far, about one-and-a-half crore loans have been sanctioned and people have been given loans worth more than Rs 4 lakh crore without any guarantee.

The 'Pradhan Mantri Gramin Sadak Yojana' was started by late Prime Minister Atal Bihari Vajpayee, but even after so many years, all the villages of the country have not been connected by roads. In 2014, when I reviewed the situation, only 57 per cent of the villages had been connected by roads. Through concerted efforts and within three years, 80 per cent of villages have now been connected by roads. Now the government is working at a fast pace to connect 100 per cent of the villages through the road network.

The emphasis of the government is on encouraging the Dalit and backward classes living in remote areas of the country to take up self-employment. So when we launched the 'Stand Up India' programme, we decided that every bank should offer loans to at least one SC/ST person in the family through this scheme.

Social rights are not a matter of lip service, but a matter of commitment for the government. The new India I am talking about is also what Babasaheb dreamt of. India with equal opportunities and equal rights for all, India free from the shackles of the caste system, India moving forward through the power of technology and India's inclusive development based on the concept of '*Sabka Saath, Sabka Vikas*'.

Let us all take a pledge to fulfil Babasaheb's dreams. May Babasaheb give us the strength to fulfil these resolutions for the year 2022. I end my speech with this wish.

□

National Memorial to Comprehend Babasaheb's Vision

—Narendra Modi

First of all, I heartily congratulate 1.25 billion countrymen for receiving today a priceless gift in the form of Dr. Ambedkar National Memorial. I feel fortunate to dedicate this memorial built in the memory of Babasaheb to the nation. Today the country is celebrating *Vaisakhi*; today also happens to be the anniversary of the Jallianwala massacre. Today I pay heartfelt tributes to every freedom fighter who was martyred at Jallianwala Bagh 99 years ago. After Independence, many governments were formed and a lot of time has passed, but the task which should have been fulfilled decades ago is now being done today. Babasaheb spent his last days here; that is why this national memorial has been built in the name of Babasaheb and it is a heartfelt tribute to him on behalf of the country. I commend the Ministry of Social Justice and Empowerment and the concerned departments for completing this task. I salute every worker who has toiled and shed sweat in its making. Built at 26, Alipore Road, this monument is a symbol of the extraordinary life of an extraordinary man. People will

---

* Speech on the occasion of inauguration of Ambedkar National Memorial on 13th April, 2018.

be able to understand Babasaheb's life and his outlook in a better way after visiting this place. This monument is made in the shape of a book, which is the Constitution of India and the sculptor of this book is Dr. Babasaheb Ambedkar. Today's new generation will be able to understand the details of Babasaheb's life with the help of the exhibition put up here when they visit this monument. Our government is fortunate to get the opportunity to develop five important places related to Babasaheb's life and which I will always remember as five pilgrimage sites. Babasaheb's birthplace, located in Mahu, Madhya Pradesh, his place of education located in London, the place of his initiation in Nagpur, Chait Bhoomi located in Mumbai, and his place of salvation in Delhi as this national monument. These shrines are not just made of bricks, but are living institutions and are the top centres of thought.

Discussion on the construction of this memorial started during the government of revered Atalji, but after the formation of the Congress government, files related to the subject were kept aside. Then in the year 2014, after the formation of the NDA government, we decided to open these files. Laying the foundation stone of the memorial, I had said, on 26 March, 2016, that I would like to inaugurate it before Babasaheb's birth anniversary in the year 2018. One can understand all the issues that had to be tackled to construct this grand building on time, the resources gathered and the will of the government.

Some of you may have visited the Ambedkar International Centre at 15 Janpath. The idea of this Centre was suppressed for 22 years in 1992. Within a year of taking over, I took the opportunity to lay the foundation stone for it in April 2015 and dedicated it to the public a few months later in December. Not crying out at lack of resources and not being affected by undue pressures can become a strength for anyone. Babasaheb has given us this power through his life and now you will not find this government crying for lack of resources. His thinking and Babasaheb's life have taught us to set our goals clearly. Today you will find that social justice and equal rights for all are the basic *mantras* of every scheme of the government. The government's schemes are directed at ending the imbalance that has been existing for decades. Take the example of the 'Jan Dhan Yojana'. Even after so many years of Independence, crores of people did not have any bank account. Our government ended that lacuna. So far more than 31 crore bank accounts have been opened under the 'Jan Dhan Yojana'. Another social injustice was the lack of toilets in crores of homes. This government has constructed 7 crore toilets in the country under the 'Swachh Bharat Mission'.

In this modern era, having no electricity in one's house is the biggest form of injustice. In the year 2014, we had more than 18,000 villages without electricity. Now, most of the villages have got electricity and under the 'Pradhan Mantri Sahaj Yojana' more than four crore houses have been given free electricity connections. The 'Mudra Yojana' aimed at promoting self-employment is also ending decades of injustice. Often the poor youth had to face the problem of providing the bank guarantee to seek loans. That's why our government has provided the option to take a loan without a bank guarantee. More than 12 crore loans have been sanctioned under the 'Mudra Yojana' and now the avenues for self-employment have become easier. Under the 'Mudra Yojana', more than 2 crore Dalit beneficiaries are getting money from banks without guarantee and have become self-reliant. The government launched the 'Ayushman Bharat Yojana' in this budget. Under this scheme, the government will provide health insurance coverage to about 10 to 11 crore poor families. This means that if someone falls ill in a poor family, he gets the assurance of receiving treatment to the tune of five lakhs by paying one rupee. The government has provided more than 3.5 crore gas connections under the 'Ujjwala Yojana'. The government has increased this target to 8 crores.

The government has made continuous efforts to curb atrocities on Dalits through relevant laws. In the year 2015, the government imposed stringent action to stop atrocities on Dalits. This law has brought down the number of crimes committed against Dalits from 22 to 47, i.e. now there will be strict action in case of 47 different crimes committed against Dalits. By amending this act, the provision of non-grant of anticipatory bail to the accused persons has been kept unchanged and the compensation amount to the victims has been increased. Social rights are not a matter of conversation for this government; it is our commitment. When I talk of a new India, it is the India of Babasaheb's dreams. Dr. Ambedkar's 125th birth anniversary was celebrated in a grand manner both in India and abroad. It was celebrated in 150 countries of the world, but the attitude of the Congress towards the Dalits was highly condemnable. Despite being the first Law Minister of Independent India, Babasaheb was not included in any committee related to defence, foreign affairs, or finance. In 1951, after resigning from the Council of Ministers, he contested elections to the Lok Sabha. Pandit Nehru campaigned against him and did not allow him to reach the Lok Sabha. Later due to the efforts of Dr. Syama Prasad Mookerjee, Babasaheb reached the Rajya Sabha. Three decades after his death, the late V.P. Singh's government posthumously awarded him the Bharat Ratna and this honour was given at the request of top BJP leaders like Shri Atal Bihari Vajpayee and Shri Lal Krishna Advani. Also it was due to the efforts of the BJP that Babasaheb's portrait was put up in the Central Hall of the Parliament. It is the result of the great work done by Babasaheb and the service rendered by him. Those who worship only one family and consider only one family as the saviour of the country are now forced to remember Babasaheb's name. This is nothing for this government to boast about, but for a commitment to social justice. It is like a devotion for us.

I want to end my speech with the wish that Babasaheb continues to bless the country and continues to bless 125 crore of our countrymen and we should continue to take inspiration from his thoughts. Once again I convey my best wishes to the countrymen for the Ambedkar National Memorial.

□

Ambedkar's Historical Revelation about Savarkar

—Lal Krishna Advani

For the first time in February 2003, a portrait of Swatantraveer (freedom fighter) Savarkar was installed in the Central Hall of Parliament. It was the NDA government at that time; Shri Vajpayee, was the Prime Minister, and Mr. Manohar Lal Joshi was the Speaker of the Lok Sabha. President, Dr. Abdul Kalam unveiled the oil painting.

For the first time in parliamentary history, the Congress party boycotted the President's programme. Since then, every 28th May, on the birth anniversary of Veer Savarkar, when MPs gather at the Central Hall to pay their homage to this great freedom fighter, Congress MPs boycott the event. The Congress party has never publicly clarified the reason for its behaviour. but the undeclared reason is that he was an accused in the Gandhi assassination case. The party ignores the fact that the court had awarded the death sentence to two and various imprisonments to others in this case, but found Veer Savarkar 'not guilty' and so acquitted him.

Two decades after the assassination of Mahatma Gandhi, Manohar Malgaonkar, a noted author of literary and non-literary books, wrote a book based on this tragedy of Indian history. The book is based on the author's interviews with the accused who escaped after serving sentences and was pardoned.

But long before the publication of this book, Malgaonkar gave this report to the most prestigious magazine of the time, *Life International*. This magazine, in its issue of February 1968, published the facts given by Malgaonkar along with photographs taken at the houses of the persons mentioned above.

In 1977, nearly thirty years after Gandhi's assassination, which shook the world, Macmillan, a London publisher, published Malgaokar's research in book form, titled *The Man Who Killed Gandhi*. I read that book after some time after its publication.

Presently, before me is the 13th edition of this book, published by Delhi-based Roli Books with the same title, but with an additional matter – unpublished documents and photographs. In this edition, the author Malgaonkar writes in his preface:

> '*In the mid-1960s, revelations made by some of those involved in the crime led to allegations that many people at responsible positions in Bombay had prior knowledge of the assassination plot, but failed to inform the police. In order to know the truth behind these allegations, the government constituted a committee under the chairmanship of Justice K.L. Kapoor. The report of the discoveries of this commission was sent to me by my friend.*
>
> '*Now I had the commission's comprehensive and incisive report and I had to prove the authenticity of Justice Kapoor's findings with my own findings. Of course, I could still write my book, but I doubted whether* 'The Man Who Killed Gandhi' *would have been a strong*

book or so long-lasting without the help of the Kapoor Commission report.

'The book first appeared when the country was in the grip of an Emergency and when merciless censorship of books was applicable. I made it my duty to take some of the things I had left out, like Dr. Bhimrao Ambedkar's secret assurance given to Shri L.B. Bhopatkar that his client Shri V.D. Savarkar was implicated in suspected killers on weak grounds. Then again other important information, such as the distorted production of a testimony by a magistrate whose duty was only to record what he was told also came to the fore in later years.'

Having put these facts and other excerpts in their rightful place, I feel that the new book is now a complete account of the conspiracy to assassinate Mahatma Gandhi.

Whoever reads this preface cannot live without appreciating how important it is for the entire nation to know what Dr. Ambedkar told Savarkar's lawyer Bhopatkar. In this context I am quoting excerpts from this edition:

'Why was the police so worried about trapping Savarkar? Is it simply because it could not do the job of arresting Nathuram Godse before killing Gandhi? Due to this, to hide its failure, the police were making an excuse that a big leader was behind it, who incidentally stood culprit in the eyes of the government of that time. Or was it the government itself, or some powerful group in it, using the police agency to destroy an opposing political organisation or at least an intense and fearless Opposition figure?

'Or was it all a manifestation of a strange kind of phobia towards India, religiousness, race, linguistics, or regionalism, which made Savarkar a natural target of revenge for certain sections of society?

'Be that as it may, Savarkar himself was alert to it; ever so careful that the government machinery would take him to court as Nathuram's accomplice that when a police team entered his house five days after Gandhi's assassination, he came to meet them and asked, 'So you have come to arrest me for Gandhi assassination?' Making Savarkar an accused in the Gandhi assassination case may have been an act of political vendetta.

'When Bhopatkar was in Delhi in connection with the case, he was accommodated in the Hindu Mahasabha office. This confused Bhopatkar when specific charges were levelled against all the other accused, but there were no definite charges against his client. He was preparing for his defence when one morning he was told that the telephone had come for him, so he went to the room where the telephone was kept to listen, picked up the receiver and introduced himself. The caller to him was Dr. Bhimrao Ambedkar, who just said, 'Please meet me this evening on the 6th mile on Mathura Road,' but before Bhopatkar would have said something, the receiver was kept down.

'That evening, when Bhopatkar himself reached the designated place by driving his car, he saw that Ambedkar was already waiting. He asked Bhopatkar to sit in his car, which he himself was driving. After a few minutes, he stopped the car and told Bhopatkar, 'There is no real allegation against your client; useless evidence has been made up. Many members of the cabinet were against it but to no avail. Even Sardar Patel could not go against these orders. But I am telling you that there is no case. You will win.'

I am glad that against the decision of the Congress party, the Speaker of the Lok Sabha, Mrs. Meira Kumar, came several times during her tenure to pay tribute to this great revolutionary. In one of my earlier blogs, I requested the Congress Parliamentary Party to reconsider their decision. Nowadays Shri Shinde is not only the Home Minister but also the leader of the ruling party in the Lok Sabha. I want the Hon'ble Lok Sabha Speaker and Mr. Shinde to take a new initiative on a clear but serious mistake.

Tailpiece

Before reading this book, I did not know where Savarkar was taken to prison by the police immediately after Gandhiji's assassination on 30th January, 1948, under the Prevention of Prisoners Act, which is one of the most malicious parts of the law, with the help of which the British ruled India.

The Bombay police raided Savarkar's house near Shivaji Park and seized all his personal letters, including 143 files and at least 10,000 letters. Malgaonkar writes: 'There was no evidence anywhere. What I found out (from these papers) was the conspirators' connection to the Hindu Mahasabha and their personal devotion to Savarkar.'

The author writes in conclusion: 'He was sixty-four years old and had been ill for a year or more. He was arrested on 6th February, 1948, and spent a whole year in prison, with the investigation and trial continuing. He was found not guilty on 10th February, 1949. The person who had spent 26 years in jail in the British Raj for the freedom struggle of India, was again in jail for a year, and that too soon after getting Independence.'

(12nd September, 2013)
(Cited from Shri Lal Krishna Advani's book, 'Rashtra Sarvopari')

□

Ambedkar: A Versatile Personality and a True Nationalist

—Dr. Murli Manohar Joshi

Dr. Ambedkar was almost forgotten for many decades after Independence, in spite of his incomparable contribution to issues pertaining to national interest, but Prime Minister Narendra Modi has started giving him the place which he deserves on the national stage. Dr. Ambedkar was rich in a multidimensional personality. He was a scholar, economist, socio-religious reformer, political scientist and constitutionalist. He is one of the great architects of modern democratic India. His relentless struggle to eradicate social untouchability and protect human rights cannot be forgotten. Actually, there are many dimensions of his personality, but I would like to discuss what Dr. Ambedkar thought about Sanskrit.

When I was the HRD Minister in the government of Shri Atal Bihari Vajpayee, issues of Sanskrit and Vedic Mathematics, etc. were raised at various levels. In this context, Dr. M.L. Singhvi had shown me the report of the Sanskrit Commission set up in 1956-57 and the main points of that report were as follows: The Bill to make Hindi an official language was not easily approved in the Constituent Assembly. Most of the people discussing this issue were tight-lipped, although some people suggested making Sanskrit the official language and Dr. Ambedkar supported it. The report further says that Naziruddin Ahmed laid the proposal to make Sanskrit the official language on the table of the House. He said that in a country where many languages are spoken, one language has to be made the language of the whole country. Then it is not necessary that it should be fair, it should not be the language of any region and it should be same for all, only then should it be accepted. By this, not a single area will be benefitted and the other sector will not consider itself crippled. Sanskrit has such potential. Laxmikant Maitre moved an amendment motion to make Sanskrit the official language in place of Hindi. He told the gathering that if Sanskrit is accepted as an official language, the psychological complexities created in the language will disappear.

There was a report titled '*Ambedkar: On the Official Language of India*' referring to a newspaper in *Sanskrit Patrika* published in May 2001 by the National Council for Education Research and Training. It was written that the Law Minister of India Dr. Ambedkar is among those who are in favour of giving Sanskrit the status of the official language of the Union of India. The Press Trust of India's (PTI) reporter questioning this, asked Dr. Ambedkar, 'What is wrong with Sanskrit?' The amended bill to give Sanskrit the status of the official language of India will be considered by the Constituent Assembly when the question of official language comes up in the House. The Amendment Bill states that the official language of the Union should be Sanskrit. It would be interesting to know that in support of making Sanskrit the official language, Dr. Ambedkar wanted the Executive Committee of the All India Scheduled Castes Federation to pass a resolution on 10th September, 1949, but that motion was withdrawn due to threats of protest by the younger members of the Executive Committee. The Amendment Bill introduced by Laxmikant Maitre, unfortunately, fell through after a heated debate, thus leaving Babasaheb's dream of uniting India in the thread of linguistic unity unfulfilled.

In my view, Babasaheb was very serious about making Sanskrit the official language because he knew that once it was approved, the bitterness that would arise during the discussion on the official language in the Constituent Assembly would end. Babasaheb wanted to free India from a linguistic war. At the same time, he wanted to keep the common Indian connected with the store of knowledge present in this ancient language. Dr. Ambedkar's attachment to Sanskrit was not just a pretense. His eagerness to know the truth of European theories regarding Aryans and non-Aryans, high and low castes, aroused his interest in Sanskrit. For this, he studied many fundamental sources including the *Vedas* with an open mind. He did not limit himself to Vedic literature, but also studied the *Zend Avesta* (Parsi scripture). Dr. Ambedkar says that the evidence from *Zend Avesta* shows that the word *varna* was related to a class of people who followed a particular custom. It had nothing to do with colour. The essence of the main points of Western theories is as follows: *Vedas* do not know about any race like Arya. There is no evidence in the *Vedas* that the Aryans invaded India and conquered those believed to be the original inhabitants of India. There is no evidence regarding the racial distinction between Aryans and other peoples. The *Vedas* do not agree that the Aryans differ from other people in appearance.

Dr. Ambedkar further says that 'if anthropometry is the science that tells the race of a person, then the study of other sections of Hindu society through anthropometry proved it wrong that the so-called untouchables are different from the

Aryans and Dravidians. It states that the Brahmins and the so-called untouchables belong to the same race. If Brahmins are Dravidians, then they are also Dravidians. If Brahmins are Nagas, then the so-called untouchables are also Nagas.' According to Dr. Ambedkar, the racial theory of untouchability not only negates the theory of anthropometry but also does not get much support from the facts which are prevalent about the culture of India, the race of the people, etc. Dr. Ambedkar's conclusions are irrefutable, but unfortunately, they are most often overlooked by those who vehemently claim to follow his ideas. We should not deny the reforms in Hindu society advocated by Babasaheb. He supported giving Sanskrit the status of an official language and showed the courage to oppose the rotten caste system. Along with this, other wrong practices of Hindu society were also opposed by him.

In this background, Prime Minister Narendra Modi's effort to convey Dr. Ambedkar's ideas to the younger generation in their entirety is commendable. I think higher educational institutions should come forward for this.

□

Babasaheb Ambedkar: A Rajarshi

—Rajnath Singh

Babasaheb Dr. Bhimrao Ambedkar was the architect of the Indian Constitution – the constitution which we have adopted and has been contributed by many great men. The role played by the Constituent Assembly under the chairmanship of Dr. Rajendra Prasadji, whatever is to be appreciated, is insufficient. An important role as the chairman of the Drafting Committee was of Dr. Ambedkar, whose 125th birth anniversary we are celebrating. The biggest achievement of Dr. Ambedkar's birth anniversary is that today we are discussing the commitment to the Constitution of India in this temple of democracy. Our country became independent on 15th August, 1947. At that time it was divided into 565 princely states. Sardar Vallabhbhai Patel played an important role in the merger of these princely states with India, but it was necessary that when we got a form of India, then there should be some binding substance which could keep India connected. Our holy book, which plays a powerful and effective role as this binding substance, is the Constitution of India. Dr. Bhimrao Ambedkar, the chairman of the Drafting Committee, played an important role in its creation. Despite how much neglect, disdain and

* Speech of Shri Rajnath Singhji in the Parliament on the eve of the 125th Jayanti of Dr. Ambedkar

humiliation he faced in his life, despite being hurt, he did the work of presenting an objective point of view for India.

Dr. Bhimrao Ambedkar never said that we are being neglected in India. He also received education from abroad. He still said that 'I will remain in India and play an important role in making India a strong nation.'

Babasaheb Bhimrao Ambedkar succeeded in executing several difficult tasks. About 7,435 proposals were received, out of which more than 5,100 proposals were to be scrapped and after that, 2,431 proposals were approved. As a result, the nature of our constitution is in front of us. If Sardar Patel was a unifying force in this country, then Babasaheb acted as a binding force for this country. While discussing the commitment of the constitution in the House, I would like to recall another great man. He was the first Prime Minister of the country, Jawaharlal Nehru. His contribution was great in strengthening democracy in this country. Many people try to present Babasaheb Bhimrao Ambedkar in common parlance as a Dalit leader, but in my view, he should not be seen from this narrow perspective. The kind of role he has played to maintain the unity of India, Babasaheb Ambedkar is indeed a *Rajarshi*.

Babasaheb played an important role in the development of labour rights and labour welfare in this country. Babasaheb emphasised the minimum wages of the workers, provident funds for the workers, and equal communication between the worker and the owner. I want to mention here that Dr. Ambedkar planned to set up the Central Waterways Irrigation and Navigation Commission. The plan for Damodar Valley Project, Hirakud Project, or any other water project is the brainchild of Babasaheb. Along with giving a constitutional framework, he also formed the basis for an economic structure for the country.

At the time of setting up the Reserve Bank of India, the suggestions of Dr. Ambedkar given to the Hilton Young Commission were made the basis. Not only this, he wrote a thesis '*National Dividend of India*' during research at Columbia University. He was the architect of the creation of the Finance Commission of India along with the Reserve Bank of India. He wrote this thesis in 1924, in which he gave the concept of the Finance Commission and on the basis of that concept, Finance Commission was established in India. He stipulated reservation for the purpose of achieving equal status for all and he believed that reservation is a political necessity. In my opinion, the reservation system given by Babasaheb Bhimrao Ambedkar was given very thoughtfully. It should not be diluted under any circumstances.

Babasaheb had envisioned an ideal society and when our constitution was made, he took three words from the French Revolution – liberty, equality, and fraternity. Dr. Ambedkar was so impressed by these words that he included them in the Preamble of the Constitution of India. The Preamble is considered the soul of the constitution. There should be no change in this and our commitment to the Constitution of India should remain, but unfortunately, the 42nd Amendment took place and the words 'socialism' and 'secularism' were added. Babasaheb Ambedkar did not use the words 'socialism' and 'secularism' probably because he believed that it is already contained in the basic nature of India. It does not need to be mentioned separately in the Preamble of the constitution. The first word of the Preamble is sovereign, and India is the only country where it exists in its original form despite facing many storms.

Considering all these things, Ambedkar did not mention some things at that time, but today we can claim that if anyone has the world's oldest sovereign civilisation, then it belongs to

India. The second word he used is 'democracy' and the fact that Indian society is fundamentally democratic is accepted by all. The third word that Babasaheb used is 'republic'. He knew that the republic established by Saint Basavanna in the 12th century in South India is the world's oldest republic, which would not be found in any other part of the world. As far as the word 'socialist' is concerned, the intention behind it was that there should be economic equality and it is present in our culture. That's why he didn't use the word. In today's politics, the word 'secular' is being misused the most and India's society is secular in itself. That's why Babasaheb did not use the word 'secular' in the Preamble of the constitution. I can say this about the secular character of India – whether it is a Parsi society or a Jewish society, they get the most respect in India.

As far as Muslim society is concerned, there are 72 *firkes* in this society and if 72_out of these 72 people live in any country, then it is India. Babasaheb knew this reality, so he did not use the word 'secular' in the Preamble. All I can say is that the Preamble of the constitution is not the soul of the constitution but a permanent reflection of the soul of India and we should understand this reality. The Constitution of India is flexible, the Constitution of India is strong and the Constitution of India is workable. I think the constitution should be taken as a holy book. Babasaheb believed that the Constitution of India was not just a written document, but it was such an effective tool that it could provide justice to all sections of society.

Dr. Bhimrao Ambedkar provided fundamental rights in the constitution with the aim of giving a defined life to every Indian. The Constituent Assembly, through Articles 14, 15, 16, 17, and 18, provided the right to equality; Articles 19, 20, 21, and 22 granted the right to freedom; Articles 23 and 24 ensure the right against exploitation, and Articles 25, 26, 27, and 28 provide the right to freedom of religion. The right to constitutional remedies has been provided in Article 32 to protect the fundamental rights of the individuals.

The nature of the Indian Constitution is unitary as well as its character is federal. The current Central Government, respecting the federal system in the country, has increased the revenue share of the states from 32 to 42 per cent. Babasaheb Ambedkar also believed that social unity is absolutely necessary for a democratic India to flourish. Under Articles 29 and 30, minorities have the right to voluntarily set up institutions under social and educational rights.

Babasaheb Ambedkar, while talking about women's empowerment, emphasised on equal rights for women and men and gave social security to women by giving rights to adoption and property right. It is the result of our Prime Minister's commitment to the constitution that 'Beti Bachao, Beti Padhao' has been taken as a national programme.

Inspired by the economic vision of Babasaheb, the Central Government started the 'Pradhan Mantri Jan Dhan Yojana', so that the welfare of the underprivileged, downtrodden, backward and poor sections of society could be done. Today, more than 99.7 per cent of households have opened accounts in banks. From the point of view of social security, 'Atal Pension Yojana', 'Pradhan Mantri Suraksha Bima Yojana', and 'Jeevan Jyoti Yojana' have been initiated. For the skill development of the people living in rural areas, the government has started the 'Deendayal Grameen Kaushal Yojana'. With the aim of Ambedkarji's concept of equality and taking everyone along, our Prime Minister is committed in every way towards 'Sabka Saath, Sabka Vikas'. We want to build such an India that even a child born in the hut of the poor should not be left behind by chance and fate, and for the creation of such an India, we are moving forward with the concept of 'Sabka Saath, Sabka Vikas'.

With these words, in the end I express my reverence and respect to Babasaheb Bhimrao Ambedkar, as well as to all the respected members of the Constituent Assembly.

□

Our Commitment to fulfil the Dreams of Dr. Ambedkar

—Thawar Chand Gehlot

Today we are discussing, while expressing commitment to Dr. Bhimrao Ambedkar, the architect of the Constitution of India and the constitution made by him. Ever since the Constitution of India came into force in the country, first as Bharatiya Jana Sangh and now as Bharatiya Janata Party, we are following it in letter and spirit. Dr. Bhimrao Ambedkar played an important role in writing the Constitution of India. On 26 November, 1949, the constitution was completed under his chairmanship and he submitted the constitution to the then government. This was his noteworthy contribution, but the government did not give him the importance which he deserved. His oil painting was not installed in the Central Hall of Parliament until 1989. Honouring Ambedkar with the 'Bharat Ratna' and installing his oil portrait were done at the behest of Atal Bihari Vajpayee and Lal Krishna Advani.

There are allegations against us that we are anti-Ambedkar. Let me tell you, in the morning prayers of Rashtriya Swayamsevak Sangh, the name of Ambedkarji is taken along

* Speech of Thawar Chand Gehlot, Minister of Social Justice & Empowerment on the eve of the 125th Jayanti of Dr. Ambedkar

with that of other great men. Among those great men included are Ambedkar, Tagore, etc. When Ambedkar contested the Lok Sabha elections, the Congress opposed him; at that time, it was Dattopant Thengadiji, an RSS Pracharak, who played an important role in the labour sector and took the responsibility of campaign for him as his election agent. They say that we do not respect the constitution, whereas we literally follow the Preamble of the constitution word by word, so that the integrity and unity of the nation remain intact. It is for the same reason Shyam Prasad Mookerjee sacrificed his life.

When Article 370 was being introduced, Ambedkar was against it, but it came into force on the basis of the majority, though it was written that Article 370 will be temporary. As a result of Article 370, if the Parliament of India makes any law, then it won't be applicable on Jammu & Kashmir. A person cannot go there and build a house, cannot be a permanent resident and cannot contest the elections as a voter. Congress says, 'We have done it to bring harmony; we have done it for the unity of the country, to strengthen it.' But, whether this is a strengthening work or not, it should be considered and agreed that Article 370 should be abolished as soon as possible.

There is a provision to introduce a Uniform Civil Code in the constitution. The Supreme Court has also advised introduction of a uniform civil code. I demand that Uniform Civil Law Code should be implemented. In 1985, in the Shah Bano case, the Supreme Court ordered alimony for Muslim women, but the Rajiv Gandhi government amended the constitution to make it ineffective. They say that there is no unity in the country, that there is no harmony. This has happened because of their wrong policies. Everyone remembers the Emergency in the country, when the work of destroying democracy was being done. That too happened during the Congress rule, even though the 42nd Amendment was made in the constitution.

Not only this, the term of the Lok Sabha, which was set for five years, was increased to six years and all of this happened on 18th December, 1976, when most of the MPs and leaders were put in jail. Many leaders, like Babu Jagjivan Ram left the Congress, on being upset with the with the attitude of centering the power in family (mother and so).

Prime Minister Shri Narendra Modi gave me the responsibility of the Ministry of Social Justice and Empowerment and said that whatever values and places are related to Ambedkarji, memorials have to be built there and they have to be made memorable. 26, Alipur Road, where Babasaheb used to reside, was a private property. During Atalji's government, the Government of India bought it and declared it a memorial. Narendra Modi's government decided that a grand monument shuld be built there at a cost of one hundred crore rupees. It has been decided to build the Ambedkar International Study Centre, Research Centre at 15, Janpath, where the Ambedkar Foundation's office is located, at a cost of 195 crore rupees. Ambedkar was born in Mahu. His father was a Subedar in the army and Babasaheb was born in the same quarter his father had been allotted in the army. A grand memorial worth Rs 14 crore was built there by the BJP government. For the last nine years, the Madhya Pradesh government organises the *Mahakumbh* on the birthday of Babasaheb. Along with this is Nagpur *deekshabhoomi*, which was strengthened by Nitin Gadkari as Public Works Minister of Maharashtra. The BJP-Shiv Sena government did the work of expanding the *Chait bhoomi*, where Ambedkar was cremated, by acquiring that land.

That land was worshipped at the hands of Narendra Modiji and 400 crore rupees is planned to be spent on this scheme. Chicholi is a village near Nagpur where all the material belongings of AmbedkarjI – the typewriter with which he typed the Indian Constitution and other material – have been kept there. The BJP-led government has approved an amount of 700 crore rupees to built a memorial thera.

Apart from this, in the years 1921-22 and 1923, when Ambedkar went to London to study, the BJP-Shiv Sena government of Maharashtra bought the house where he lived and the Prime Minister has announced to convert it into his memorial.

Let me remind my Congress friends that during their tenure, there was a controversy on reservation for Scheduled Castes/Scheduled Tribes, who once belonged to the Hindu religion. They used to fall under the Scheduled Caste category. When they converted to some other religion, the Congress was of the opinion that they should still be given the status of Scheduled Caste. For resolving this matter, Congress filed a writ in the Supreme Court of India. Apart from this, the Sachar Committee and Ranganath Mishra Commission were constituted and it was said that some percentage should be deducted from the SC/ST quota and given to the converts, but Dr. Ambedkar, the architect of the Constitution of India, and others had already discussed this subject. These discussions took place in 1936, 1948, 1952, and 1956, and it was said that the status of Scheduled Caste status could not be granted to the converts because the system of reservation for the Scheduled Castes came into being due to untouchability, due to social and educational backwardness. When someone converts to a religion, there is no such atmosphere of untouchability in that religion. It is written in the Constitution of India that there is a provision to ban conversion, but you are trying to promote conversion. By doing this, you are compromising the unity and integrity of the country.

Our Prime Minister has decided to celebrate the 125th anniversary of Dr. Ambedkar with great pomp. A committee has been formed under the chairmanship of the Prime Minister. We have chalked out the programme for the whole year. The message to celebrate today as Constitution Day in all the states of the country was dispatched by the Government of India. Postage stamps and coins have been issued on Babasaheb Ambedkar. A hundred students of the country were sent abroad to places wherever Dr. Ambedkar Sahib had gone to study.

Children in batches of 25 were sent to London, to Columbia, to Washington and to America. Seminars and discussions were organised. I can say that Babasaheb was respected the most by Hon'ble Atalji and Modiji. We are in favour of reservation. Let me remind you, the Second National Convention of Jana Sangh was held in Indore where we proposed that we respect the Constitution of India and Babasaheb Ambedkar. When Narendra Modiji was the Chief Minister of Gujarat, he placed the Constitution of India on an elephant in Surendranagar district and led a procession of one lakh people.

I want to convey that to bring social harmony to the country and strengthen its unity and integrity of the country, we are fulfilling our responsibility to follow the Constitution of India. In its tenure of one-and-a-half years, our government has to its credit many achievements. Our ministry has chalked out many plans for the Scheduled Castes, the Backward Classes, the persons with disabilities, the eunuch caste, the nomadic caste, the senior citizens and plans to do a lot more. We just have to learn that Babasaheb Bhimrao Ambedkar should be respected and we must abide by the constitution framed by him.

□

Commitment to Dalits, Tribals and Forest Dwellers: A Tribute to Babasaheb

—Yogi Adityanath

The year 2019 has been significant in many ways as the Uttar Pradesh legislature discussed important issues related to the nation and society through a special session held this year. In the year 1959, through the 8th Amendment of the constitution, the system of reservation provided under the constitution for Scheduled Castes and Scheduled Tribes was extended for 10 years. It was felt that the expected development and representation of these classes had not taken place.

After Independence, according to the constitution of the country, a meaningful effort was made to offer benefits of government schemes to every section, without any discrimination, so that all become a part of the mainstream in development of the society and the nation. Plans progressed at every level and to take these plans forward, it was felt that every 10 years we need to discuss this subject in the legislature to give due representation to the communities belonging to the Scheduled Castes and Tribes. We are here today to give

* Speech of Shri Yogi Adityanath in the Uttar Pradesh Assembly

our support to the ratification of the 126th Amendment Bill of the constitution through this special session. Reservation will continue till 25th January, 2020. This special session has been called so that the Uttar Pradesh legislature can give its ratification to this Constitutional Amendment Bill to extend it for the next 10 years from 25th January, 2020 onwards.

When the country became independent, at that time, the population of Scheduled Castes was 5 crore 13 lakhs and the population of Scheduled Tribes was 1 crore 91 lakhs. As per the 2011 Census, the population of Scheduled Castes was 20 crore 13 lakhs and the population of Scheduled Tribes was 10 crore 45 lakhs. As many as 84 Scheduled Castes and 47 Scheduled Tribes members have been elected in the Parliament from all over the country. In the State Legislative Assemblies, 614 Scheduled Caste and 554 Scheduled Tribe members were elected from their respective states. Naturally, this Constitution Amendment Bill also needs the support of the state legislatures. From this point of view, we have to send this support at the level of the Uttar Pradesh legislature from here.

After Independence, the Central Government, under the leadership of Prime Minister Narendra Modi, has done the work of realising the dream of Babasaheb Bhimrao Ambedkar without any discrimination. The Prime Minister has developed *panchteerthas*, a holy site associated with Babasaheb Bhimrao Ambedkar. Babasaheb's birthplace in Mahu, Madhya Pradesh has been developed as a pilgrimage site by building a grand memorial to him. The building in England where Dr. Ambedkar had earned his higher education, has been bought together by the Government of India and the government of Maharashtra. Along with building a memorial of Babasaheb Dr. Ambedkar in this building, arrangements for offering residence and scholarships to students going to England were made by Prime Minister Narendra Modi.

The place where Babasaheb Ambedkar breathed his last in Delhi was bought by the NDA government which was elected under the leadership of Shri Atal Bihari Vajpayee. The Central Government under the leadership of Prime Minister Narendra Modi has developed it into a holy pilgrimage centre by building an international centre there. A grand memorial was built at Nagpur. This work was completed by the government of the then Chief Minister of Maharashtra Devendra Fadnavis, under the leadership of Prime Minister Narendra Modi. The Prime Minister Narendra Modi-led government has done the work of awakening a ray of hope among the underprivileged of the world by developing the holy place 'Chaitya Bhoomi' at Mumbai as it was associated with Babasaheb Ambedkar.

Prime Minister Narendra Modi, after taking oath as Prime Minister on 26th May, 2014, had clarified the government is not meant for any person, caste, faith, religion, region or any language, but for India, for Indianness. He said that we will 'work for the villages of India, for the poor of India, for the Dalits of India, for the tribals of India, for the forest-dwellers of India, for the women of India and for the development of every section of India. He has also done it during his five-and-a-half-year reign.

When Narendra Modi was sworn in as the Prime Minister, there were three crore homeless families in the country. The work of providing a house each to two crore such families was completed under the 'Pradhan Mantri Awas Yojana'. There were 10 crore families without a toilet in their house. The Prime Minister has done the job of giving one toilet to such families through the 'Swachh Bharat Mission'. There were three crore families who did not have their own electricity connection. Under the 'Saubhagya Yojana', work has been undertaken to provide electricity connections to these families. Under the 'Ujjwala Yojana', the Prime Minister provided LPG connections to 8 crore families. Under 'Ayushman Bharat' health insurance cover of Rs 5 lakh is being given by the Prime Minister to 50 crore poor and underprivileged people.

Scholarships to Scheduled Caste and Scheduled Tribe students were not given in the year 2016-17 due to some unknown reason, while the state government of that time kept on beating its drum by proclaiming that it was working for the welfare of the poor and the downtrodden. When our government came to power in March 2017, we took up the task of giving full scholarships to Scheduled Caste and Scheduled Tribe students. Whatever the government of our party says, it does it. We have done what we have said. We have never discriminated in the name of the scheme, the name of caste, region, religion, or language. This government is fully committed to ensuring that people get the rights given under the constitution without any discrimination.

We are all gathered here today to support the Constitution Amendment Bill passed by the Parliament of the country. Parliament has passed it unanimously. By passing this unanimously, the Uttar Pradesh Legislative Assembly can associate itself with its commitment towards the poor, the downtrodden, the Dalits, tribals and forest-dwellers. With the view of fulfilling this, I will appeal to the entire house that this resolution should be passed unanimously. There should be no politics over this issue.

The year 2019 has been an important year from the point of view of the legislature of Uttar Pradesh. Many special sessions were convened this year. A special session was convened on 2 October on the occasion of the 150th birth anniversary of Bapu.

It was at this session that the Sustainable Development Goals (SDGs) were discussed and tributes were paid to Gandhiji. After this, a special session was convened on 26 November on

Constitution Day as a tribute to Babasaheb Ambedkar. Today is the last working day of the year 2019. By convening this special session on this last working day too, we have taken a step forward in building the India of Dr. Ambedkar's dreams.

□

Ambedkar's Constitution Unites and Integrates All

Dr. Bhimrao Ambedkar, popularly known as Babasaheb, was a social reformer, a Dalit icon, a world-class jurist and the principal architect of the Indian Constitution. He was born on 14th April, 1891, in a poor Untouchable family in Mhow, Madhya Pradesh. He was the fourteenth child of Ramji Maloji Sakpal and Bhimabai. They belonged to the Hindu Mahar caste and were called Untouchables who were discriminated for being economically and socially weak. Ambedkar's father was a Subedar in Mhow Cantonment and always encouraged his children to study and work hard. At the behest of one of his Brahmin teachers, Mahadev Ambedkar, who had a special affection for Ramji Sakpal, Babasaheb removed Sakpal from his name and added Ambedkar, which was based on the name of his village, Ambavade. Ambedkar became a nominated member of the Bombay Legislative Council in 1926. In 1927, he decided to start a massive movement against Untouchability. He fought for the rights of Untouchables to enter Hindu temples as well as throw open public resources of drinking water to all the people of the society through public movements and processions.

Due to the increasing popularity and public support of Dr. Ambedkar, he was invited to participate in the Second

Round Table Conference held at London in 1931. In 1936, he founded the Independent Labour Party, which was successful in winning 15 seats in the 1937 Central Assembly elections. He published his book titled, *The Annihilation of Caste* in 1937 and it was based on his paper written in New York. In this book, he criticised the caste system existing in Hinduism and strongly condemned the decision of the Congress to call the people of the Untouchable community as 'Harijans', the word composed by Gandhiji.

In Independent India, he became the country's first Law Minister in the Congress-led government and was appointed chairman of the Constitution Drafting Committee on 29th August, 1947, and on 26th November, 1949, the Constituent Assembly adopted the constitution. On this occasion, Dr. Ambedkar said, "I feel that the constitution is achievable and flexible but at the same time it is strong enough to keep the country united in both peace and wartime. In fact, all I can say is that if something ever went wrong, it would not be because our constitution was bad, but the man who used it was bad."

In 1951, he resigned from the cabinet in protest against the stopping of his draft Hindu Code Bill in Parliament. The draft called for gender equality in inheritance, marriage and economic laws. Ambedkar was nominated to the Rajya Sabha as an independent candidate in 1952 and remained a member of the Upper House until his death. The legacy of Dr. Ambedkar's political and social reforms had a profound impact on modern India. After Independence, his social and political thinking has found respect. His thinking is displayed through today's social and economic policies, education, legislation and affirmative actions.

Dr. Ambedkar, the architect of the Constitution of India, had many dreams. He wanted India to be a caste-free, industrialised nation and a democratic country. He was a very talented student. He was educated at Columbia University and the London School of Economics. He received doctorates in economics from both these universities. He gained fame in his research work on law, economics and political science. Early in his career, he was a professor of economics. He was a great economist for the country and openly opposed the caste system. He dreamed of an economically strong India, free from casteism, but the dirty politics of India established him as the leader of the Dalit society instead of making him the leader of the society.

Ambedkar's services to the country have many dimensions, but at the time of making the constitution, he had expressed his apprehensions regarding the problems of caste and language. He had warned that the constitution can only provide provisions for the organs of the state, such as the legislature, executive and judiciary, but the operation of these organs depends on the people and on the political parties to fulfil their aspirations. He was clearly seeing that in the future, taking advantage of the benefits of democracy, political parties with different conflicting ideologies may lead to unrest due to caste and sect politics. Babasaheb would have never dreamed that a university campus in the nation's capital would raise slogans of '*Bharat tere tukde honge*', '*Insha Allah*' or '*Afzal hum sharminda hai tere kaatil zinda hai*'. If at the time of partition, a complete transfer of the Hindu-Muslim population between the two countries had been accepted, then this would not have happened today, but Ambedkar's words were not accepted, as a result of which, even after the passage of seven decades, there is an atmosphere of communal unrest in the country.

Some people forcibly try to downplay him by calling him a Dalit leader and alleging that he resigned from the Nehru cabinet, angered by the government's attitude towards Dalits. But the reality is that Pandit Nehru did not listen to Dr.

Ambedkar regarding Article 370 and despite many protests, Article 370 was inserted in the Constitution. Through the second Hindu Code Bill, he wanted to give women their rights, but the bill introduced by him was not passed in the Lok Sabha. So he resigned from the cabinet. It is a different matter that the supporters of women's empowerment do not take the name of Dr. Ambedkar but in the entire parliamentary history of India, Dr. Ambedkar and Arif Muhammad Khan have been the two ministers who resigned from the cabinet for the rights of women. The only difference was that the Hindu Code Bill introduced by Babasaheb could not be passed due to opposition from orthodox Hindu MPs and Arif Muhammad Khan had to resign in protest against Rajiv Gandhi's government nullifying the Supreme Court's decision in the Shah Bano case in order to appease the fanatics.

Babasaheb's concept of Indianness states that we are Indians first and we are Indians in the end – if this concept had been accepted by all, then the map of the country would have been different. Unfortunately some people say that we are Hindu or Muslim first and then Indians. Now a section of the society is coming which says that religion comes first and the country later. This situation is dangerous for the country. Troubled by issues of political contradictions, Dr. Ambedkar founded the Buddhist Society of India in 1955 and embraced Buddhism in a public ceremony at Nagpur with millions of his supporters. On 6th December, 1956, he fell into a deep slumber at Delhi. Babasaheb's house at 26th Alipur Road in Delhi was converted into a national monument, which was inaugurated by the Prime Minister Narendra Modi. He will always be remembered for the work he has done for the country.

□

Ambedkar's Dream: Equal Opportunities for Underprivileged Society in India's Governance

Whenever, in the history of independent India, there is mention of important dates like 15th August, 1947 and 26th January, 1950, mention will also be made of one other important date – 26th November, 1949, the day when we received our constitution due to which India attained the status of a democratic republic. Babasaheb Ambedkar was the creator of the constitution that we adopted. Being the chairman of the Drafting Committee, his diligence and hard work resulted in the creation of the Constitution of India in which the Preamble forms the basis of the Indian system of governance. Our Prime Minister Narendra Modi is following the path shown by Dr. Ambedkar to establish an egalitarian society by working on the *mantra* of 'Sabka Saath Sabka Vikaas'. Even as Chief Minister of Gujarat, on the occasion of the celebration of the Constitution Day, he organised a procession on foot with lakhs of people following behind him, with the Constitution of India kept on the back of an elephant. He has been a firm believer in the fact that it is due to the contribution, sacrifice and dedication of Babasaheb that he could become the Prime Minister of India. Beginning his life as a tea-seller to becoming the Prime Minister of India, his journey was possible only because of the Constitution which was framed through tireless hard work and dedication of Babasaheb.

A few of my friends who continuously keep chanting the importance of secularism allege that the Rashtriya Swayamsevak Sangh (RSS) and Bharatiya Jana Sangh have been the opponents of Babasaheb are being proved totally wrong in their views. When Dr. Ambedkar was contesting the elections in the Lok Sabha, it was the Congress which fiercely opposed him and tried its best to not let Babasaheb succeed in the elections. During that time it was Dattopant Thengadiji who, as the Pracharak of RSS and known for playing a crucial role in the welfare and upliftment of the workers, took charge as Dr. Babasaheb's election agent. Moreover, Babasaheb was against the inclusion of Article 370 which was stipulated by the Congress. When the NDA government came to power under the leadership of late Atal Bihari Vajpayeeji, several welfare schemes for the welfare of Dalits and tribals were introduced. To ensure the empowerment of the underprivileged in governance, the name of the Ministry of Social Welfare was changed to the Ministry of Empowerment.

In 2003, with regards to ensuring proper marketing of the goods produced by tribals like jute, honey, rope, etc., the Tribal Cooperative Marketing Development Federation was established. Special projects were initiated for the rehabilitation of tribals, the oppressed and the downtrodden so as to provide them free education, healthcare, poverty alleviation and protection of their language. In 1999, the Vajpayee government announced a National Policy for the Welfare of Tribals and constituted a separate ministry of tribal affairs.

After becoming the Prime Minister in the year 2014, Narendra Modiji launched the 'Start-Up India' and 'Stand Up India' schemes to give an impetus to the new entrepreneurs in the country, especially those coming from underprivileged classes. Under the 'Stand Up India' initiative, instructions were issued to 1.25 lakh bank branches in the country to provide financial assistance to new entrepreneurs especially to those belonging to the SC/ST and to women entrepreneurs. During the reign of the NDA government, with the view to overcoming the difficulties faced by the entrepreneurs belonging to the deprived class, a tax benefit of 7,200 crore rupees per annum was given to the MSME sector. The amount under the 'Mudra Yojana' has now been increased to 1,22,000 crore rupees. Besides this, to overcome the problems faced by entrepreneurs belonging to the deprived society in the MSME sector in availing the credit, the government has launched several schemes. Under the Credit Guarantee Scheme Fund for Micro and Small Industries, guarantee cover for collateral-free loans up to one crore rupees has been sanctioned. In the field of employment generation in rural and urban areas, the government has given a big relief to the unemployed youth belonging to Scheduled Castes and Scheduled Tribes through several schemes, including the Credit-linked Capital Subsidy Programme and the Prime Minister Employment Generation Programme (PMEGP). Margin money subsidy at the rate of 20 per cent of the project cost is provided to SC/ST entrepreneurs in urban areas, while this subsidy is 35 per cent for rural entrepreneurs. Scheduled Castes and Backward Classes have a large participation in rural and traditional industries. To make it more competitive, the Scheme of Funds for Regeneration of Traditional Industries (SFURTI), launched in the year 2005-06, has been restructured. This scheme aids socially backward (SC/ST/OBC) entrepreneurs to set up micro and small enterprises in the manufacturing and service sector. Aspire, a scheme for the promotion of innovative rural industry and entrepreneurship, promotes Livelihood Incubators through the National Small Industries Corporation Khadi Village Industries and Coir Board. Credit Growth Guarantee Scheme for new entrepreneurs belonging to Scheduled Caste and Scheduled Tribe was launched on 10th February, 2015, with a budgetary provision of 200 crore rupees. The Prime Minister's thinking behind this scheme is that due to lack of money and self-confidence, the youth belonging to the poverty-stricken or deprived society are unable to start any enterprise despite possessing the necessary talent. This scheme provides an opportunity to work in addition to instilling confidence amongst the youth of the underprivileged society.

Apart from this, various welfare schemes that are being run by the Ministry of Social Justice and Empowerment under the Government of India for the development of Scheduled Castes include:

1. For educational empowerment, pre-matric scholarships and post-matric scholarships, along with National Fellowship, Excellence in Education, National Overseas Scholarship and free coaching are being provided for the higher education of Scheduled Caste students.
2. Financial assistance is provided in the form of loans to Scheduled Caste families, margin money at low-interest rates and subsidy through the Scheduled Caste Development Corporation in the Centrally-sponsored schemes for the economic empowerment of Scheduled Caste people. Presently Scheduled Castes Development Corporation is functioning in 23 states and in four Union Territories.
3. The Scheme of Special Assistance to Scheduled Castes Sub Plan (SCSP) is a Central sector scheme. Under this, a cent per cent grant is given to states and Union Territories in addition to the Scheduled Caste sub-

plan. The main objective of this scheme is to emphasise the economic development of the Scheduled Caste population so that they can be brought above the poverty line through self-employment and training.

4. Central assistance is provided to states/UTs for implementation of the Protection of Civil Rights Act, 1955 and the Scheduled Castes and Scheduled Tribes (Prevention of Atrocities) Act, 1989, under the schemes of social empowerment and integrated area development. The Scheduled Castes and Scheduled Tribes (Prevention of Atrocities) Amendment Rules, 2016, have been notified in the *Gazette of India: Extraordinary*. These amendments include payment of relief amount to victims in a phased manner, provision of payment to victims of atrocities, their family members and their dependents within seven days and completion of investigation and filing of charge-sheet in the court within 60 days, depending on the nature of the offence and the amount to victims of atrocities has been increased to 85,000 rupees. Impressed by Babasaheb's ideology of equality and taking everyone along, our Prime Minister is completely committed to 'Sabka Saath, Sabka Vikas' and 'Sabka Vishwas'. We want to build such an India where a child born in a poor family is not a victim of opportunity and fate.

In accordance with Dr. Ambedkar's conception of egalitarian society and equal representation of all, it is the result of the determination of the Prime Minister that the President of the country, the Prime Minister and the Speaker of Lok Sabha belong to either a tribe or a backward society. A moment came in the history of this country when Babu Jagjivan Ram could have become the Prime Minister of the country, but despite the rigorous efforts made by the Jana

Sangh faction of the Janata Party, a Dalit could not become the Prime Minister of the country because the Congress got the Lok Sabha dissolved by a crooked trick. It is hoped that Prime Minsiter Modi will one day fulfil Gandhi's and Bababsaheb's dream of providing equal opportunity to the backward society in Indian governance.

□

Dr. Ambekdar's and Mahatma Gandhi's Ideology on Hindu Vision (Philosophy)

The strange irony of Indian history is that Babasaheb Ambedkar and Mahatma Gandhi had been fighting to put an end to the stigma of conservative exploitation and caste system in their own ways, but the views of both of them were considered to be conflicting. Although the objective of both was same, the approach and medium for achieving that objective were different. Gandhiji's ideology evolved through the frame of a Sanatani Hindu, who is against social exploitation. He did not have feelings of resentment or hatred towards anyone in his heart, whereas Dr. Ambedkar surely had anger towards conservatism and social management of the Hindu religion due to some of his experiences in the past though that cannot be termed as a feeling of hate. Due to his harsh, fierce and determined views, the Congressmen initially kept a distance from him and called him loyal to the British Government, a supporter of Western thoughts and imperialism. Senior Congress leader Smt. Meira Kumar, daughter of senior Congress leader Babu Jagjivan Ram, has said on many occasions that Independence of the country was not the priority of Dr. Ambedkar, though this is not true. His patriotism was no less than that of any other leader of this country. For the establishment of social equality, he wanted to directly fight the atrocities committed by the upper-caste Hindus against the Dalits which had been going on for two thousand years along with the fight for the independence of the country. He was influenced by the ideas of Jyotiba Phule, Govind Ranade, Gopal Ganesh Agarkar, etc. and was determined to stand up against the injustice meted out to the downtrodden. In 1916, his article written on the caste system was an open-thought platform for the struggle against the prevailing caste system in society. He wanted to completely eliminate the evil of high and low based on birth and that is why he is considered to be a staunch enemy of Brahmanism. He always viewed the liberal theory of the upper-caste Hindus with suspicion. He believed that the Dalits themselves would have to fight against Brahmanism and end it. In fact, he was such a thinker who came out of the Independence movement and whose prime concerns pertained to the Dalit class and the caste system.

Gandhiji was not so strong on the caste system and untouchability, but in his thinking, a constant opposition to inequality and exploitation on the basis of caste is reflected. He clearly revealed his views in an essay titled 'Brahmin and Brahminetara' in the issue of *Young India*, November 1920. He said that the British government had given a political colour to the Brahmin and non-Brahmin questions to weaken the Independence movement. This apprehension of Gandhiji proved to be true and the *Firangis* baked their political bread by initiating the fight between Brahmans and non-Brahmins. Dr. Ambedkar completely disagreed with Gandhi's views and he firmly believed that Gandhi's love for Dalits was a pretense. The opportunistic British government took full advantage of this position of Gandhi and Ambedkar. In 1932, the British reserved some seats in the legislature for Muslims and other minority communities. Muslims, Sikhs, Christians and Parsis were already considered to be minorities but with the inception of this new law, the Dalit class was also included in the minorities, indicating the fact that preparations were being made to separate them from Hinduism. The Congress was aware that having a separate electorate would give birth to a new and separate politics of the Dalit class, which was the reason why all the nationalist leaders opposed the politics of separating the Depressed Classes from the rest of the Hindu society. When Gandhi became acquainted with this policy in the Yerwada Jail, he opposed it as in his opinion, this was a direct attack on the Indian Independence movement. He believed that this was the groundwork for letting Untouchables remain Untouchables forever and a conspiracy to push people toward religious conversions.

Upon realising the severity of the situation, Gandhi went on a fast unto death on 20th September 1932. Many political parties opposed it by calling it a political stunt of Gandhi, but the strike received tremendous support from the public. On this occasion, Babasaheb Ambedkar supported Gandhi and finally an agreement was reached, which is known as the Poona Pact. Under this Poona Pact, reservation was arranged for the Dalits by abandoning the idea of a separate electorate. Gandhi then started the Harijan *yatra* from Wardha in November 1933 and toured the country for nine months, from place to place. During his tour, he used to inform his supporters, "Either they should end Untouchability or they should remove me from their midst." Babasaheb had witnessed with his own eyes how the reactionary forces joined hands with the British government with the sole objective to reduce Gandhi's influence and get the Temple Entry Bill passed. As a matter of fact, there is a deep similarity between Gandhi and Ambedkar, despite their ideological differences. Not merely this but also both are complementary to each other despite some conspirators trying their best to portray and prove them as contradictory.

Dr. Ambedkar acquired higher education at Columbia University and from London. In America, he became well acquainted with American apartheid, racism and separatism. The French Revolution deeply impacted him, so he continued to fight for equality, fraternity and fundamental rights. Although the British used to embrace the downtrodden class, treat it equal and not believe in Untouchability by keeping the doors to employment always open, still, Babasaheb knew the intention behind this kindness offered to the Dalits by the British. He knew that the Untouchables could not prosper by converting to Christianity. Their good was possible only if Untouchability was removed from Hindu society. He often used to say that if Hinduism is to be saved, then end Brahmanism in Hindu society. He was in love with the *Upanishads* which were based on liberty, equality and universal brotherhood. Babasaheb said, "I do not like what some people say, that we are Indians first and Hindus afterward or Muslims afterward. I do not want that our loyalty as Indians should be in the slightest way affected by any competitive loyalty, whether that loyalty arises out of our religion, our culture, or out of our language. I want all people to be Indian first, Indian last and nothing else" (*Dr. Babasaheb Ambedkar: Writings and Speeches*, vol. 2, p. 195).

Regarding his attachments towards India and Dalits, he said, "I say this, that whenever there has been a conflict between my personal interests and the interests of the country as a whole, I have always placed the claim of the country above my own personal claims. I say this to this House as strongly as I possibly can. Whenever there is any conflict of interest between the country and the Untouchables, so far as I am concerned, the Untouchables' interests will take precedence over the interests of the country. I am not going to support a tyrannising majority simply because it happens to speak in the name of the country. I am not going to support a party because it happens to speak in the name of the country. I shall not do that. Let everybody here and everywhere understand that is my position. As between the country and myself, the country will have precedence; as between the country and the Depressed Classes, the Depressed Classes will have precedence – the country will not have precedence" (*Dr. Babasaheb Ambedkar: Writings and Speeches*, vol. 2, p. 258).

He understood that a change in the status of Dalits was necessary for the establishment of an egalitarian society. This is the reason why he, along with economists, continued to work on the origin of 'development' effect of the caste system. Dr. Ambedkar did not consider Manu, who was the founder of the Hindu legal system and the creator of *Manusmriti*, as the creator of the caste system, as he believed that caste existed before Manu. Therefore, it would be a mistake to say that the caste categories were created by the scriptures and the *Smritis*. These scriptures and *Smritis* provided the religious and social basis to the caste system by giving power to the Brahmins.

The Brahmins did not have the power to impose the caste system on the non-Brahmins. Their priesthood rested on the king. The myths of Rama and Krishna were not borne out of the racist colour theory; behind them was the philosophy of cow-feeding culture. That is why Babasaheb says, "All people are hybrids in terms of lineage; cultural unity is due to their homogeneity. Considering this fact, I can dare to say that no country can compete with India in cultural unity, despite its hybrid composition. There is not only a geographical unity in it, but there is a deeper and more fundamental unity than that. Cultural unity pervades the whole country, from one end to the other, but it is because of this cultural uniformity that it becomes very difficult to solve the mystery of caste" (*Dr. Babasaheb Ambedkar: Writings and Speeches*). Forming the Bahishkrit Hitkarini Sabha, Dr. Ambedkar did not rely at all on the emulation theory of historian Arnold Toynbee; he became active in churning the ocean of religious philosophical concepts of our country and found that "Hindu philosophy teaches the principle of the all-pervading soul and the *Gita* teaches not to discriminate between Brahmins and Chandalas."

While Gandhi supported *varna* system, Ambedkar completely rejected it. The two differed at this point and never reached an agreement. That is why Dr. Ambedkar burned the *Manusmriti* and remained adamant about the establishment of a single-class society. He believed that it was impossible to get rid of the caste system without putting a whammy on the religious principles of the caste system. He also challenged the economic theory of Marxism. In his words, "Socialists assume that the current system of European society is the principal source of wealth-power. But this idea is a hoax. Religious philosophical ideologies have played a major role in the context of India and Indian Marxists have been unable to understand this role. Whichever side you go, you have to fight the demon of casteism. Unless you kill this demon, no one can bring economic or political change (*Babasaheb Dr. Ambedkar: Writings and Speeches*, p. 47). Dalits were surrounded by religious discipline and were deprived of higher education, culture and philosophy. As a result, they became incapacitated and were trampled on by foreign invaders. The caste system played a deep role in the roots of our defeat.

Gandhiji expressed his regret about the stigma on the forehead of Hinduism and said, "According to my interpretation of *varna*, *varna dharma* is not practiced in Hinduism today. Those who have the name Brahmin have stopped teaching education; they have started doing more business. The same is true of some other *varnas* as well." In fact, Gandhi was not as anxious to end the caste system as Dr. Ambedkar was. Once Gandhi even said, "I don't want *swaraj* for the Depressed Classes at the cost of any other class. I don't think it will be *swaraj*. I am of the view that the moment India is purified, it will be free; not before" (*The Collected Works of Mahatma Gandhi*). Babasaheb Ambedkar, who disagreed with these views of Gandhi, never cooperated with Gandhi because his view was very clear that Untouchability cannot be abolished from this country without completely destroying the caste system. For this reason, instead of considering the British rule in India as a true devil, he considered the caste system to be a true devil. Dalits had hailed the British as liberators from the age-old tyranny of Sanatani Hindus. They fought battles against Hindus, Muslims and Sikhs for the British and won the kingdom of India for them.

Ideological differences emerged between Gandhi and Ambedkar on the occasion of the Round Table Conference, but Ambedkar did not bow down. Gandhi said, "Separate voter list and reservation cannot wash away the stigma which is a taint on Sanatani Hindus and not on Dalit castes" (*The Collected Works of Mahatma Gandhi*).

Gandhi used to say, "In my opinion, the cause of our misfortune is not the caste system, the reason for our slavery is our greed and our neglect of essential qualities. I believe that the caste system has saved Hinduism from disintegration." Unlike Gandhi, Ambedkar believed the caste system to be the cause of India's decline and slavery. Gandhi used to support the *chaturvarnya* division of *Gita* as a right and this support of Gandhi was not acceptable to Ambedkar. So, one day, he broke away from Hinduism and took refuge under Buddhism.

Babasaheb said, "Why did our country lose its independence time and again? Why were we caught in foreign rule every day? Because this country never stood united before the enemy. Only a small section of the society came forward and the one who defeated it, became the winner. The main reason for this is the destructive caste system of the Hindus." Due to this opposing ideology, Gandhi and Ambedkar could never unite. In Dr. Ambedkar's speech titled, 'Abolition of Caste System' in 1936, Gandhi said, "The *varna* system teaches us that we should all follow the profession of our forefathers and earn our living. It determines our duties, not our rights." But Babasaheb continued to be uncomfortable with these remarks of Gandhi and eventually left Hinduism to become a Buddhist.

The truth is that the goal of both Gandhi and Ambedkar was human welfare. Though both had their own views on the *varna* system and had their own arguments to justify them, both are relevant to us for the establishment of liberty, equality and love.

□

Partition of Country and Dalit Society

In 1947, as a matter of fact, there was a communal division based on the Hindu-Muslim religions, but the society which suffered the most during the division, was the Dalit society. That is why Dr. Ambedkar at that time kept emphasising complete population transfer, but today, when Prime Minister Narendra Modi's NDA government, through the Citizenship Amendment Act, made a provision to give citizenship to the minority communities of Pakistan, Bangladesh and Afghanistan, in which the majority consists of Dalits, all the Opposition parties including the Congress oppose it. It is absolutely essential to know about the way Mohammad Ali Jinnah sowed this seed back in 1947. Born in a Gujarati family in the Karachi district of modern Sindh province, the ancestors of Mohammad Ali Jinnah were Hindu Rajputs. Jinnah later converted to Islam and after completing primary education in Bombay, moved to Delhi to study law. After joining the Congress in 1896, instead of demanding Independence of India like the Moderates, Jinnah kept asking the British about better opportunities for good education, law, industry, employment, etc. in the country.

In 1906, the Muslim League was formed and the League started working on the concept of a new nation based on religion. Although Jinnah initially avoided joining the League, but in 1913, he too joined it. He joined and decided to lead the minority Muslims in the country. Jinnah's differences with the Congress commenced in the year 1916, when an agreement was reached between the Muslim League and the Congress. In 1918, Gandhi observed that freedom and self-governance were achievable only through the movement of truth, non-violence and civil disobedience, whereas Jinnah believed that freedom could be achieved only through constitutional struggle. In 1920, Jinnah resigned from Congress and became the president of the Muslim League. But again, after many years, he moved back to London. Thereafter, he returned to India after repeated requests from such leaders of the Muslim League – Aga Khan, Chaudhry Rahmat Ali and Mohammad Allama Iqbal and Jinnah re-formed the Muslim League in 1934. In the Central Legislative Elections, 1937, the Muslim League gave a tough fight to Congress and won a majority of Muslim-dominated seats. Then the Congress and the League decided that both would fight the British together, but Jinnah put forth a devious condition – the Congress would have a separate constituency for the Muslims and the Muslim League would be the representative of the Muslims in India.

After failed negotiations with the Congress, Jinnah's mind produced the thought that Muslims should get a separate country to protect their rights. Later Jinnah's view became absolutely certain that both Hindus and Muslims were citizens of two different countries and hence should be segregated. His view later came to be known as the 'two-nation theory' of Jinnah. In the Lahore session of 1940, a resolution was passed saying that the main objective of the Muslim League was the creation of a separate country – Pakistan. Congress did not accept this proposal and leaders like Maulana Abdul Kalam Azad strongly condemned it, but Jinnah did not agree. In order to fulfil his dream, he gave a helping hand to Britain during

World War II and also opposed the Quit India Movement of 1942. At the same time, Dr. Ambedkar said that there should be complete relocation of the population of both the countries when the country was being divided on religious lines because he knew that in the event of the formation of Pakistan, the rich peoples would stop the Dalits to fulfil their needs and later they would definitely have to face inhuman torture. Jinnah understood this apprehension of Ambedkar; therefore, he, in a very smart move, involved the then veteran Dalit leader Jogendra Nath Mandal in the campaign to create Pakistan. Later, with the help of Mandal, he actively started settling Dalits in Pakistan. Jinnah's only purpose behind doing this was to increase the population in pursuit of fetching a greater portion of land during partition in the name of Dalits and Muslims.

Before Independence, Jogendra Mandal was considered the main face of the Dalit movement like Dr. Ambedkar and he was extremely popular amongst the people of Dalit society living in Bengal and Bangladesh. By taking Mandal along with himself to achieve his objective, Jinnah tricked and misled the Dalits to create Pakistan. For the first time in the history of the politics of the country, Jogendra Nath Mandal propagated the Dalit-Muslim alliance, but this experiment was the biggest mistake of his life. At his behest, the Dalits, who had left for Pakistan, had to bear the atrocities of the Muslim community residing in Pakistan till they converted to the Muslim religion. After partition, Mandal not only became the first Law Minister of Pakistan, but also the chairman of the committee that wrote the constitution of Pakistan. However, in 1950, Mandal resigned from the Government of Pakistan and came back to India, never to return to Pakistan.

Jogendra Nath Mandal lived in the eastern part of India and emerged as a new hope for the Dalit community. After his early education, he studied law at the University of Calcutta and started litigating in the Calcutta High Court in 1935. But, he soon realised that he could not do anything for his Dalit society without gaining power or an intrinsic role in the government. Then he entered politics and joined the Congress. In 1937, he was nominated for the district council and later he was elected as a member of the Bengal Legislative Council. By the year 1940, Mandal realised that there was no desire to do anything for the Dalit society on the agenda of the Congress. In the meantime, he got in touch with Dr. Ambedkar and then along with his colleagues, he joined Dr. Ambedkar's Indian Scheduled Caste Federation on 19th July, 1942. Subsequently, he established the Scheduled Caste Federation in Bengal and took the work of Dr. Ambedkar in his own hands. Meanwhile, the disappointment received from Congress and the strong desire to do something for his own community led Mandal to get in touch with Mohammad Ali Jinnah before entering the Muslim League.

At this time, Dr. Ambedkar was disturbed by the manner Dalits were represented in the making of the constitution of the country. On the other hand, Nehru and the Congress Committee had arranged to deter any member of the Dalit society to win the elections. Even Dr. Ambedkar was not likely to be elected. In such a situation, Mandal invited Dr. Ambedkar to file his nomination from Bengal and explained to all the Scheduled Caste MLAs of Bengal to ensure Dr. Ambedkar's victory. Ultimately, Dr. Ambedkar won the elections with the efforts of Mandal. Meanwhile, Mandal's contact with Jinnah continued to flourish over time and Mandal got deeply preoccupied with the dreams that Jinnah showed to him – the dream of the liberation of Dalits after the formation of Pakistan. Finally, after the partition on 15th August, 1947, Mandal became the president of the Constituent Assembly formed in the new country of Pakistan. Later he became the first Law and Labour Minister of Pakistan. He continued to handle this responsibility till 1950, but by then Jinnah's true picture emerged and Mandal learned to his dismay that Jinnah, who talked about Dalit welfare, was not in the least interested in curbing the atrocities committed on the Dalits in Pakistan.

After the formation of Pakistan, the way Muslims massacred the Hindus in the country, that is, the economically and socially weak Dalits, was a genocide of such severity which Mandal could never forget as he realised the real truth behind the formation of the Dalit-Muslim alliance. His voice against this was never heard by the Islamic government. Frustrated and devastated in the end, Jogendra Nath Mandal returned to India in 1950 and lived a life of oblivion at Vangaon in West Bengal. He finally died in oblivion on 5th October, 1968, regretting his actions.

During his last days, Jogendra Nath Mandal realised that through the Muslim-Dalit political alliance, he had committed the biggest mistake of his life by relying on Muslims. Non-Dalit and wealthy Hindus migrated from East Pakistan to West Bengal, that is, India, but 32 per cent of the Hindus remained behind till 1950 and out of them, the Dalits constituted 90 per cent of the total Hindus. Today, instead of 32 per cent of Hindus in Bangladesh, only 8.5 per cent of Hindus remain, of which 90 per cent are still Dalits. They were not even allowed to escape from Pakistan and were forcefully made to serve as slaves. That is why Dr. Ambedkar was in favour of bringing the Hindus and Sikhs left behind in Pakistan to India, when the country was being partitioned. This was the sole reason why he mentioned the citizenship law in the constitution as simply and clearly as possible. He knew how the Dalits would be harassed, oppressed and humiliated in Pakistan. When they did not spare their country's Law Minister and constitution maker, Dr. Ambedkar tried persuade the entire Dalit society to leave Pakistan and come to India to live here in peace. If the religiously persecuted Dalit Hindus of Pakistan and Bangladesh could not return to India, then where else could they go?

If the Dalits of India oppose the Citizenship Amendment Act under the influence of some Dalit leaders and Leftists, then it will be fatal for their community only.

□

Citizenship Amendment Act: A Tribute to Babasaheb

Prime Minister Narendra Modi, after taking oath as the Prime Minister of India for the second time, abolished Article 370, which had been continuing for the seven decades after Independence. In the second session of the House, he attempted to fulfil Dr. Ambedkar's dream by enacting the Citizenship Amendment Act, which Babasaheb had been advocating at the time of the partition of the country on communal lines, but Pandit Nehru and his associates had turned down. What was particularly irksome was the continued support for the creation of Pakistan by Leftists and Muslim organisations, including the Congress, under the divisive policy of the British. The Hindu Mahasabha, along with the Rashtriya Swayamsevak Sangh and other nationalist organisations were opposed to the partition on religious lines. What was worse that Dr. Ambedkar had accepted this demand in 1940 itself because he had learned that it was no longer possible for Hindus and Muslims to live together within one nation. Therefore, for this reason, he supported complete displacement and transfer of both the communities to their respective nations. He proposed complete relocation of the population along with the partition of the country to avoid riots during the partition. He said that the Muslims should go to their newfound country because he knew that the rich people belonging to Pakistan would stop the Dalits to fulfil their needs and later exploit them on religious grounds. Now, Prime Minister Narendra Modi, with the object to free the Dalits from their despicable life, has enacted the Citizenship Amendment Act.

Dr. Ambedkar had prepared a detailed action plan for the population transfer and this he placed before everyone in 1940, through his book, *Pakistan and Partition of India*. He had seen how, after the Ottoman Empire, the population had been divided between Greece, Turkey and Bulgaria; in a similar manner the population transfer could be brought about in India as well, but the Congress rejected Babasaheb's plan because it was still fantasising of bringing about Hindu-Muslim unity. Dr. Ambedkar had foreseen that after the formation of Pakistan, Hindus would be persecuted and a system for the safe evacuation of Hindus had to be devised before partition occurred. But no one accepted Dr. Ambedkar's plan. The result was that after the partition, in 1947, a large number of the Hindu population, mostly the Dalits, stayed behind in Pakistan. But, after a few days, it became difficult for them to live due to the deadly attacks on them and their forcible conversion to Islam. Lakhs of Hindus, who opposed conversion, were killed and their properties confiscated. Due to the lack of complete exchange of population, many Muslims remained behind in India. Their population has increased to more than 200 million today while the number of Hindus left in Pakistan is just a few thousands in comparison to their population being more than 10 million at the time of partition. Hindus living in Bangladesh and Pakistan had to suffer the consequences of not insisting on a full population swap before the partition. As result, many Muslims remained behind in India and whose population has increased to more than 200 million today.

Even today, many people are opposed to the Citizenship Amendment Act as they allege that Prime Minister Narendra Modi and his government want to tear apart the constitution formulated by Babasaheb, who has given a systematic and analytical description of the political attacks by Muslims in his book, *Babasaheb Dr. Ambedkar: Speeches and Writings*, vol. 8, p. 248). Reflecting critically on the Muslim ideology, Dr. Ambedkar advised a detailed analysis of the basic ideas and principles of Islam, on the basis of which the politics and fundamental behaviour of the entire Muslim world are determined. He said, "How the Muslim mind will work and by what factors it is likely to be swayed will be clear if the fundamental tenets of Islam which dominate Muslim politics and the views expressed by prominent Muslims bearing on Muslim attitude towards an Indian Government are taken into consideration" (*Babasaheb Dr. Ambedkar: Writings and Speeches*, vol. 8, p. 292). He adds, "Among the tenets, one that calls for notice is the tenet of Islam which says that in a country which is not under Muslim rule, wherever there is a conflict between Muslim law and the law of the land, the former must prevail over the latter and a Muslim will be justified in obeying the Muslim law and defying the law of the land."

Referring to the principles influencing Muslim politics and ideas, Dr. Ambedkar wrote on p. 204: "According to Muslim Canon Law, the world is divided into two camps, Dar-ul-Islam (abode of Islam) and Dar-ul-Harb (abode of war). A country is Dar-ul-Islam when it is ruled by Muslims. A country is Dar-ul-Harb when Muslims only reside in it but are not rulers of it. That being the Canon Law of the Muslims, India cannot be the common motherland of the Hindus and the Musalmans. It can be the land of the Musalmans – but it cannot be the land of the 'Hindus and the Musalmans living as equals'. Further, it can be the land of the Musalmans only when it is governed by the Muslims. The moment the land becomes subject to the authority of a non-Muslim power, it ceases to be the land of the Muslims. Instead of being Dar-ul-Islam, it becomes Dar-ul-Harb."

According to Dr. Ambedkar, this view of Muslims strictly affects the conduct of Muslims. During the Khilafat Movement of 1920-21, not only did a large number of Muslims follow the Masjid rule, but also left their homes in India and went to Afghanistan (*Babasaheb Dr. Ambedkar: Writings and Speeches*, vol. 8, p. 295). On p. 293, he has stated that in order to get rid of the body from Dar-ul-Harb, there is a rule to wage *jihad* (crusade) in Muslim mosques. According to this, Islamic rule should resort to use of arms until the non-Muslims bowed down before them. Muslims can, not only declare *jihad*, but can also take the help of any foreign Muslim power to make *jihad* successful, and if any foreign Muslim power considered the declaration of *jihad*, then that power can also help to make its effort successful (*Babasaheb Dr. Ambedkar: Writings and Speeches*, vol. 8, p. 285).

This has been ingrained in the minds of Muslims and that is why they chant the slogan, 'One-umbrella Islamism'. Islam considers Hindus to be infidels (*kafir*), that is, inferior to them. Dr. Ambedkar has written to what extent the Muslims will obey the dominion of a government, controlled and ruled by Hindus. The country which is ruled by infidels is called Dar-ul-Harb and in such a situation, it will not be acceptable to Muslims to consider themselves important citizens of a country ruled by non-Muslims (*Partition or Thoughts on Pakistan*). He writes that the cruel methods adopted by the Muslim invaders and the Muslim rulers who ruled over India left behind a second crop of bitterness, due to which the bitterness between Hindus and Muslims increased to such an extent that it could not be pacified even during British rule. Muslim invaders destroyed many Hindu temples, forcibly converted Hindus to Islam, looted their property, made them slaves and humiliated their women. Apart from this, Muslim invaders came to North India and spread all over India, replacing the original Aryan civilisation of India with Islam, due to which the religious and political sphere of Muslims became widespread. Had these invaders gone back after destroying Hindu temples and looting property, it would not have had such harmful consequences (*Babasaheb Dr. Ambedkar: Writings and Speeches*, vol. 8, p. 63).

Dr. Ambedkar has also mentioned that after the formation of Pakistan, Hindus would be captured in Pakistan and so, before this partition, there should be a system to bring them all safely out of Pakistan. When Pakistan becomes a Muslim-majority State and has sovereign rights in internal and external affairs, it will be out of the control of the Central Government. In such a situation, there will be no question of interference from any external power for the Hindu minorities. Thus, the condition of Hindus in Pakistan will be the same as that of Armenians under Turkey, or Tsarist Russia, and Hindus under Nazi Germany, and this situation will be intolerable for Hindus (*Babasaheb Dr. Ambedkar: Writing and Speeches*, vol. 8, p. 65).

This was the sole reason why he wanted complete population transfer at the time of partition. The famous writer Koenraad Elst, while describing the Congress mentality, has written: "There was a big difference of opinion between the Congress leadership and Dr. Ambedkar regarding the Partition. Both Nehru and Gandhi till the very end made unusual compromises to deny the permanent and irrefutable facts of Partition and indulged in delivering shameful exemptions. Gandhiji and Nehru humbly surrendered themselves to the Muslim goons."

Dr. Ambedkar put forward a permanent form of a clean agreement, but Gandhi-Nehru refused to give up their faulty views and destroyed Hindu-Muslim unity. At the same time, even after the partition of India and the full acceptance of two separate nations, they strongly opposed the proposal of relocation of population, which led to serious consequences for the Hindus living in Pakistan and Bangladesh.

After 72 years of India's Independence, Prime Minister Narendra Modi has taken this historic decision to grant citizenship of India to the Hindu minorities residing in the neighbouring countries and this would be a befitting tribute to Dr. Babasaheb Ambedkar.

□

Leftist Ideology and Ambedkar

Ever since the Central Government passed the Citizenship Amendment Act 2019, since then, parties like Congress, TMC, Samajwadi Party and BSP have been mobilising the people against the Citizenship Amendment Act (CAA)/National Register of Citizens (NRC). Their stand is understandable since the vote bank of these parties depends on Muslim, Christian and Dalit votes. One thing which really surprises is that in the name of protecting the Constitution, all the Leftists of the country are standing in opposition to C.A.A/N.R.C. The agitation by Leftists against the National Register of Citizens and the Citizenship Amendment Act needs to be studied with reference to Babasaheb's views. It has been the character and modus operandi of the Leftists to oppose the civilisation, the culture and the society of India while living in India. This fact was well realised by Babasaheb.

Now the question arises as to which reasons Dr. Ambedkar was opposed to the Left and used his power and influence to save the Dalit society of India from the clutches of the Left. He said, "The Left, meaning Marxism, considers religion as the opium. For Marxists, religion is a pain – the elimination of religion, or the end of the illusory happiness of the people, as the Marxists say." In short, religion is a mine of sorrow according to the Left, whereas Babasaheb Dr. Ambedkar says that religion is not opium. Whatever good things are in me or whatever benefits are being received by society through my education and initiation, they have all been possible only because of my religious feelings. I want religion, but do not want any kind of hypocrisy or pretense in the name of religion (*Dr. Babasaheb Ambedkar: Life and Mission*, p. 305).

Dr. Ambedkar did not agree with the anti-religious and irreligious approach towards life. According to him, religion is a part of the social life of man and the heritage of the individual. The life of a person, honour, respect, etc. are all associated with religion. Babasaheb had a firm belief in the social power of religion and that power lies in religion in the form of an organised system of belief and practice (*Critics of Dr. Ambedkar*, p. 32). Attacking the Left, Dr. Ambedkar clearly said, "Some people think that religion is not necessary for society. I do not accept this view. I consider the foundation of religion to be essential for the life and behaviour of society" (*Dr. Ambedkar ka Dharmadarshan*, p. 70).

While hitting at the roots of the materialistic theory of the Left, Dr. Ambedkar emphasised that where is the joy in material things which is in the religious pursuit? Material production cannot solve all human problems. Religion is essential for human happiness and peace. Man cannot survive on bread alone. Religion infuses hope in human beings and frees them from despair, leading them to taking suitable and beautiful actions. He further highlighted that there was no justification to belong to a society that emphasised only on bread. Man is a social animal, who can hardly live without religion and culture. Dr. Ambedkar believed that religion originated for the service of human beings. Therefore, human beings should not be used to maintain the continuity of redundant traditions of religion. It is an effective means of social upliftment. Religion should be judged by social norms based on the morality of the society.

If religion is adopted for the happiness and peace of man, then there can be no other additional criterion for evaluating religion.

The Leftist notion of morality, which protects the interests of the proletariat group, is not acceptable to Dr. Ambedkar because it creates conflict and discord and anything that creates discord and conflict in the society cannot be called moral. It is because every class and caste in the society establishes its own morals, which are unacceptable to other classes. On that account, Dr. Ambedkar expressed his faith in certain moral principles which, in a true sense, are equally applicable to all races and similar countries. Babasaheb believed that general principles of morality were essential for a just social order in society. The general, universal and sacred rules of morality will, not only protect good human beings, but will also protect the weak and also the interests of individual development. Therefore, morality should be all-encompassing and there should be no moral norms made for the benefit of a particular class. Dr. Ambedkar believed that the protection of morality of a particular class is totally unjustified. In its place, only morality determined by keeping in mind the interests of the society as a whole, is desirable. Dr. Ambedkar says that the morality of a particular class leads to social upheaval and that morality, which is based on common ideals, is capable of bringing the upliftment of people towards social cooperation and coordination. The hope for humanity lies in the fact that the spirit of fraternity should be made universally effective because the brotherhood of mankind is another name for human morality (*Dr. Ambedkar: Buddha and His Dhamma*, p. 323).

Dr. Ambedkar did not accept the explanation of the economic power of the Left. According to the Left, man is an economic animal, but Babasaheb did not agree with this.

He says that socialists always ignore the problems arising out of the social system and want to apply the economic interpretation of history to Indian conditions, just as their European peers do. Leftists say that man's activities and aspirations are bound by economic facts and that property is the only source of power. That's why they preach that political and social reforms are a huge illusion and that equitable distribution of wealth and economic reforms should be given priority over all other reforms. In fact, economic motivation is not the only economic motivation. No student of human society can accept that economic power is the only power (*Babasaheb Sampoorna Vangmay*, vol. 1, p.62).

Babasaheb Ambedkar asked a question from the Left: 'Can you accomplish economic reforms without bringing in social reforms?' The Left in India seem to have never considered this question. Dr. Ambedkar believes that the social status of an individual is often the source of power and this is hundred per cent true in India. His authority depends on his social status just as the influence of sages can be seen on the general public. Why do millionaires in India believe in the words of *sadhus* and mystics? Lakhs of poor people go to Varansi and Rudraprayag to earn merit. Religion has always been the source of power in the history of India (*Babasaheb Sampoorna Vangmay*, vol. 1, p. 62).

There is also a view of Marxism that history is determined by the economic condition and economic production of the country and society. Babasaheb did not reject the role of economic forces in human life, but he did not believe that only economic means determined the direction of history. In fact, man is responsible for a just and unjust social order. For any system, it is necessary that man should serve the interests of society (*Ranade, Gandhi and Jinnah*, p. 5).

In fact, the entire Leftist political theory was invalid

according to Babasaheb because he had unwavering faith in democracy. He was a staunch supporter and lover of individual liberty and used to oppose the fundamental principles of the Left by saying that my people have been Dalit, exploited and oppressed till today; now there is an awakening in them and due to which it is natural for them to harbour resentment and enthusiasm. "I no longer want my society to fall prey to the Left and become victim to the same." Ambedkar stands as a barrier between the Dalits and the Leftists.

□

Article 370 of the Constitution of India and Ambedkar

Since the day of India's Independence, Article 370 has been the subject of discussion. The NDA government under the leadership of Atal Bihari Vajpayee was often accused of not raising crucial issues like Article 370, Common Civil Code and Ram Mandir, while these subjects were the main issues of Bharatiya Jana Sangh and Bharatiya Janata Party since the time of Dr. Syama Prasad Mookerjee. In the government led by Prime Minister Shri Atal Bihari Vajpayee, the BJP had only 182 Lok Sabha members and had to run a coalition of 23 parties to attain a majority, which prevented him from raising these core issues. As far as Article 370 is concerned, it was from the very beginning opposed by the founder of Bharatiya Jana Sangh, Dr. Syama Prasad Mookerjee. He undertook to fight against it as he felt that it was Article 370 which divided into several small pieces. He also went on a hunger strike in order to oppose it. When he went to Jammu & Kashmir to agitate against it, he was arrested there and died under mysterious circumstances in police custody on 23rd June, 1953.

When the country got Independence, it was a major challenge to merge more than 560 princely states into one single nation. During this period, apart from the princely state of Hyderabad, and the state of Jammu & Kashmir, all the princely states acceded to India. It was later that through the efforts of Home Minister Sardar Vallabhbhai Patel, Hyderabad and Junagadh to were merged with India. On 26th October, 1947, Maharaja Hari Singh of Jammu & Kashmir signed the accession of his princely state to India, but there was no mention anywhere in this accession treaty that after the merger, Jammu & Kashmir would be given special status. However, the state's interim Prime Minister Sheikh Abdullah wanted the state to be designated as a state under special status.

After becoming the Prime Minister of Jammu & Kashmir on 5th March, 1948, Sheikh Abdullah held a press conference to say, "We have decided to live and die with India' though from the very beginning he had been dreaming of acquiring autonomy for Kashmiris so that they could govern as per their aspirations. On the advice of Nehru, Sheikh Abdullah took the draft to make his demand to Dr. Ambedkar, chairman of the Drafting Committee of the Constitution. Dr. Ambedkar refused this draft, saying, "You want us to build roads in the state of Jammu & Kashmir, to provide protection to it. Henceforth you are taking all the facilities from India and then demanding to have a special constitution which is different from other Indian states. If that happens, then that will lead to injustice and will be discriminatory against the rest of the Indian citizens and will be incorrect." Thus Dr. Ambedkar not only refused to draft a separate constitution for Kashmir but also said that such a provision would not be good for the country.

On receiving Dr. Ambedkar's refusal to accept the draft, Sheikh Abdullah approached Pandit Jawaharlal Nehru to seek help. Pt. Nehru decided to engage the services of Gopalaswami Ayyangar, who was a member of the drafting committee and the Diwan of Maharaja Hari Singh of Jammu & Kashmir. A heated debate ensued between Gopalaswami Ayyangar, Sardar Vallabhbhai Patel and Sheikh Abdullah over Article 370 (which was referred to as Article 306A in the draft). Ayyangar wrote in a letter to his friend, "Time is running out. I do not understand nor agree with many things." Even Ayyangar had threatened to resign from the Constituent Assembly at that time and said that this was not right.

Thus, this draft was made at Nehru's insistence and which Dr. Ambedkar, chairman of the Drafting Committee, rejected. Gopalaswami Ayyangar, a member of the Drafting Committee, wrote the draft under pressure of Nehru despite disagreeing with it. Meanwhile, Prime Minister Nehru went on a foreign tour to America and instructed Home Minister Sardar Vallabhbhai Patel to get this draft passed in Parliament. On 12th October, 1948, Sardar Patel addressed the Constituent Assembly and said, "Keeping in view the special problems that the government of Jammu & Kashmir is facing, we have made specific arrangements on the present grounds regarding the constitutional relations of the state with the Centre."

Nehru got this draft passed at the behest of Sheikh Abdullah, despite the refusal of Dr. Ambedkar and knowing very well the danger it posed. In a letter to Prem Bazaz, a leader of Kashmir, on 21st August, 1962, he said, "Article 370 will end sooner or later." It implied that he was aware that inclusion of Article 370 would prove detrimental to the country. In a state where Hindus and Buddhists have an illustrious history and where even the second Buddhist assembly was conducted, had now become a Hindu-minority state. Dr. Ambedkar had called Article 370 a betrayal to India.

On 11th September, 1964, Shri Prakash Vir Shastri presented a motion in the Lok Sabha, but the then Home Minister opposed it. After Independence, Article 370 was opposed both inside and outside the Parliament, but due to the policy of anti-Hindu and Muslim appeasement of Congress, it was retained. It was due to it that thousands of Kashmiri Pandits had to flee form their homeland and till today, they are compelled to live the life of displaced persons, away from Kashmir. No warrior of secularism ever raised his voice at the plight of Kashmiri Pandits.

Finally, Prime Minister Narendra Modi decided to abolish this much-awaited controversial Article and Home Minister Amit Shah introduced the historic Jammu & Kashmir Reorganisation Act in Rajya Sabha on 5th August, 2019. Now Article 370 of the Constitution has been removed from the state of Jammu & Kashmir. Additionally, the bifurcation of the state of Jammu and Kashmir into two Union Territories of Jammu-Kashmir and Ladakh has been welcomed all around. Some separatists and communalists who were engaged in establishing Kashmiriyat are now burning with rage at their failed plans. With the abrogation of Article 370, Jammu & Kashmir has been linked with the whole country, opening new avenues for development of Kashmir as well for the youth seeking employment in new ventures. Now the youth of the state can enter the All India Services, State Administrative Services, Central Services, Police Services, etc. without any discrimination as they will now have to compete with entrants from other states as well.

Prime Minister Narendra Modi has done a commendable job by abolishing Article 370 for which the founder of Bharatiya Jana Sangh, Dr. Syama Prasad Mookerjee had to sacrifice his life. It is in fact a true tribute to Babasaheb Ambedkar and Dr. Syama Prasad Mookerjee. Even as an economist, Dr. Ambedkar did not want to deprive Jammu & Kashmir of development activities and that is why he continued to oppose Article 370, which would have cut off the state from the rest of the country. Finally Prime Minister Modi has been able to put an end to this problem which had been persisting like a thorn piercing the country's unity for the past 72 years.

□

Ambedkar's Contribution to Women's Empowerment

Today every person in the Indian society is talking about women's empowerment, but it was Dr. Ambedkar who took the lead in this matter with his liberal views. He showed the way to liberating women from the clutches of age-old customs and practices. He believed that before Manu wrote the *Manusmriti*, the position of women in India was very respectable and women had been granted the right to education and participate in religious activities.

Babasaheb's fight pertaining to women's empowerment was witnessed in 1942, where, in a conference of women belonging to the oppressed class, he said, "The progress of a community is measured by the progress of the women of that community." The constitution of the country was finalised in three years, but the women's fight for their rights still continues. Indian society is largely patriarchal. He publicly burnt the *Manusmriti* to celebrate women's empowerment in a symbolic manner. He set an unmatched example by introducing the Hindu Code Bill in Parliament. Unfortunately, when this Bill was introduced, there was a rebellion inside and outside the Parliament. Both the followers of Sanatan Dharma and Arya Samaj strongly opposed Ambedkar. A massive protest was held outside the Parliament against the Hindu

Code Bill under the leadership of Harishchand Saraswati alias Karpatriji Maharaj. Despite opposition from these staunch Hindu organisations, Dr. Ambedkar continued his fight for women's empowerment. In the second session of the All India Dalit Women's Conference, Babasaheb said, "I have been the biggest supporter of women's upliftment and freedom and I have tried my best to improve the status of women in my community. I am working towards passing the Hindu Code Bill so that it can do welfare for the complete women community. When I was considering the Hindu code, I have seen young and adult women who have been abandoned by their husbands and are given only four to five rupees monthly for their subsistence. With the passing of the Hindu Code Bill, such distressed and helpless women could, by the force of law, get divorced from such tyrannical husbands and marry again for a living. A strong feature of the Hindu Code Bill was also that the marriage of any two Hindu brides and groom, irrespective of their caste or creed, would be considered valid and the child born of that wedlock would become a legitimate shareholder in the ancestral property. Whereas centuries before, children born out of marriages between conflicting *varnas*, castes and sub-castes were not considered legitimate children to get a share in ancestral property. Hindu Code Bill, not only entitles a Hindu male-child to be adopted, but a girl-child can also be adopted, and additionally, it enables her to inherit the property of the adoptive parents."

The Hindu Code Bill was a revolutionary step for the empowerment of women socially and economically. This bill was drafted especially for the advancement of Hindu women. It was formally introduced in the Lok Sabha on 5th February, 1951 but due to widespread opposition, this bill could not be passed in Parliament in the said year but later, this bill was passed by the Parliament in different parts, such as Hindu

Marriage Act, Hindu Succession Act, Hindu Minority and Guardianship Act, Hindu Adoption and Maintenance Act. All these acts were passed in the Parliament between 1952 and 1956; however, the foundation stone for all of these acts was laid by Dr. Babasaheb Ambedkar in the year 1951 only.

With this bill, Hindu women got the right to divorce, because according to the belief of Hindu scriptures, if a woman comes out of her father's house on a palanquin (*doli*) to her husband's house, then she cannot leave her husband's house till her death. It was considered a sin for married women to return to their father's houses. No matter how many marriages the man entered into, the woman used to respect the husband as a God, particularly in the case of polygamy being committed by the husband, the first wife always used to get harassed, but with the passage of the Hindu Marriage Act, the condition of women improved a lot. The Hindu Adoption Act gave Hindu women the right to adopt a child and also the right to a share in the property of their parents. Apart from this, women got many other rights, such as women got the right to their earnings, the right of the daughter to be the heir and the freedom of inter-caste marriage.

The teachings of Gautam Buddha and the social work of Mahatma Jyotiba Phule had a great influence on the personality of Dr. Ambedkar. Buddhism was the first religion in human history that gave women the right to religious education and preached gender equality. Mahatma Phule did historical work for the education of women in the 19th century and his wife Savitribai Phule established the first school for the education of girls and Dr. Ambedkar considered Mahatma Phule as his guru. Dr. Ambedkar believed that democracy would only be established in the country in a true sense when women were given an equal share in the ancestral property and when they could enjoy equal rights as men.

Dr. Ambedkar organised many conferences to make women aware of their rights. He inspired women toward their rights through newspapers, like *Mooknayak* and *Bahishkrit Bharat*, etc. As Law Minister of India, where he worked for the rights of all the classes, he introduced the Hindu Code Bill for the welfare of Hindu women, due to which he had to face opposition from the conservatives.

Babasaheb Ambedkar did a commendable job in making women financially self-reliant. Today, when the Women's Reservation Bill is still under consideration in the Lok Sabha, Dr. Ambedkar's views on women's empowerment become even more relevant. Whenever any literature in the future is going to be written on women's empowerment movement in India, Dr. Ambedkar's name will be written in golden letters. To give shape to Dr. Ambedkar's views towards women and his vision of economic self-reliance of women, Prime Minister Narendra Modi launched several schemes in the field of entrepreneurship to ensure the representation of women in every field. For economically weaker women, the government provides loans, without interest, to set up small-scale industries. Various schemes are being run by the Small Industries Development Bank of India for women entrepreneurs. Women entrepreneurs are becoming self-sufficient with the initiatives taken by the Prime Minister and that day is not far when women entrepreneurs will give tough competition to male entrepreneurs and this will be a real tribute to Dr. Ambedkar.

□

Dalit-Muslim Alliance Contrary to Ambedkar's Ideology

Babasaheb fought for the rights of the Dalits and downtrodden throughout his life. He arranged for reservation in the Indian Constitution to ensure their development, but he never tried or thought to separate the Dalit society from the mainstream of the nation. After him, Babu Jagjivan Ram, the biggest personality of the Dalit community, continued to follow Ambedkar's path and made efforts for the overall development of Scheduled Castes and to include them in the mainstream of the nation. The present Dalit leadership undoubtedly takes the name of Babasaheb, but, on the contrary, they support the policy of separatism, which is totally unfair and contrary to the interests of Dalits and the nation as a whole.

At present, many Dalit leaders, who call themselves Ambedkarites, are playing a dangerous game to exercise power, by giving the slogan of 'Jai Bhim'. They do not realise how harmful this game would prove for the Dalit society. If Indian politics falls victim to the Dalit-Muslim alliance, then the Dalit class will have to bear the maximum loss. Jogendra Nath Mandal had already experienced this bitter truth as he went to the Islamic State, Pakistan under Jinnah's delusion. During the time of partition, instead of supporting the full population transfer proposed by Dr. Ambedkar, he allowed Dalit Hindus to stay on in Pakistan and later because of his decision, they were forced to lead a neglected life. Subsequently he himself returned to India after resigning from the post of Law Minister of Pakistan and never thought of going back to Pakistan again (Dr. Krishna Gopal: *Babasaheb: Vyaktitva aur Vichaar*, p. 202). If we look at the Dalit leaders of the present era, then most of the leaders are seen shouting slogans of 'Jai Bhim' in the name of the Dalit-Muslim alliance. Among such people, Jignesh Mevani, Chandrashekhar Azad alias Ravana, BSP supremo Mayawati and those who believe in Congress ideology. Since the BJP's victory in the 2014 Lok Sabha elections and the formation of the NDA government, the Dalit-Muslim alliance has been continuously chanting where as Babasaheb continued to oppose the Dalit-Muslim alliance as also the Leftists throughout his life. In the name of this alliance, the sole purpose of all these people is to topple the NDA government and by any means restore the Left and Congress ideology to power, while the Left ideology has been completely rejected in most of the countries since the economic reforms era. In India too, the Left governments have lost elections in all the states including Bengal, Tripura and Kerala.

Kanhaiya Kumar came into the limelight by becoming the messiah of the Dalits, chanting the melody of Dalit-Muslim unity when he left no stone unturned to instigate the war against the Government of India, by giving the slogan of 'Bharat Tere Tukde Hoenge' in JNU in the name of alleged welfare of Dalits and the backwards. He continuously advocated Dalit-Muslim alliance all over the country. Today, the Delhi government has given permission to prosecute him for sedition. There is a very simple question: 'How can those who are against India be Dalit-friendly?' The direct meaning of Dalit upliftment in this country ends at protesting against the Hindus, while Ambedkar never talked about weakening or going against Hinduism for achieving the goal of Dalit upliftment. Today's Dalit agitators see no other purpose than to isolate the Dalits from the Hindu society. Today's Dalit and deprived society is increasing its participation in Indian politics. In such a situation, implicating the downtrodden and the Dalits on the issue of religion and caste is nothing but a betrayal of the Dalits.

Chandrashekhar Azad alias Ravana, who fuelled the violent dispute between Dalits and the upper castes in the Saharanpur district of Uttar Pradesh, is active in the Dalit-Muslim alliance as a Dalit leader. He argues that if the Dalits and the Muslims unite, then the problem of Dalits and Muslims will be solved, whereas Babasaheb always rejected such a Dalit-Muslim alliance. Jignesh Mevani, who came into the public eye in the year 2015, is also dreaming of crossing his political lines on the strength of the Dalit-Muslim alliance to protect Dalit interests in India. Jignesh, who came out of the Dalit movement in Gujarat, is currently an MLA. Congress seems extremely excited about Jignesh Mevani, who emerged from the movement against the unfortunate Dalit violence that took place in the Saurashtra region of Gujarat. He is an absolute opponent of the BJP. He has the support of Congress and the common man, but he is trying to make the Dalits a separatist violent group by diverting them from the path of education and development.

Asaduddin Owaisi, who is a Member of Parliament and holds the image of a staunch Muslim of Hyderabad, is also striving for a Dalit-Muslim alliance these days. Waris Pathan, belonging to the party of Asaduddin Owaisi, had threatened that 15 crore Muslims will prevail over 100 crore Hindus, but Waris Pathan is unaware of the fact that 20 per cent out of those 100 crores that he is dreaming of destroying and taking over are Dalits – the Dalits, with whom their leaders are dreaming of coming to power.

Hon'ble Kanshi Ram was known as the biggest leader and messiah of Dalits after Babasaheb Ambedkar and Babu Jagjivan Ram. It is an indisputable fact that he mobilised and instilled confidence in the Dalits and made a Dalit woman the Chief Minister of the country's largest state. He avoided opportunistic alliances throughout his life, but after his death, BSP supremo Mayawati is constantly trying to come to power with the help of opportunistic alliances. During the Lok Sabha elections in the year 2014, Mayawati was aiming to win the elections on the strength of Dalits and Muslims, but her strategy did not work. For the sake of Muslim votes in the 2019 Lok Sabha elections, she buried the guest-house incident and formed an alliance with the Samajwadi Party; yet, this time she got nothing but disappointment.

Due to Narendra Modi's progressive outlook and determination to fulfil Babasaheb's dreams, he is getting immense support from the Dalit community. Left intellectuals and Christian missionaries are exceedingly active in putting an end to this support. They are luring the Dalit community to shape a better future for them if they were to join the Muslims or if they were to adopt Christianity, whereas the reality is that their golden future can only be ensured if they continue to be part of the mainstream of the nation.

The Dalit society of the country has to understand that neither they will get any welfare nor will they get any special benefit from being either with the Muslim or Christian society. The life of Jogendra Nath Mandal, which was gifted to the Dalit-Muslim alliance, is the biggest example for us to learn from. To keep away from the Dalit-Muslim alliance experiment, we must keep in mind the suggestions made by Dr. Ambedkar. Many Dalit leaders played their respective roles in the empowerment of Dalits in Independent India and among them, Babu Jagjivan Ram, Erode Venkatanaykar alias Periyar, Kanshi Ram, and Ram Vilas Paswan were prominent. There was one commonality among all of them and it was that they never threw Dalits into the fire of violence, like today's leaders. They were comfortable with people of all castes and religions, and they had good relations with the people of Muslim society, but they never talked about any sort of Dalit-Muslim alliance to acquire political power. Babu Jagjivan Ram held the position of a minister at the Centre for more than three decades and the department in which he was a minister, strived to fulfil the Dalit representation while he attempted to bring social change in his own way. However, his opposition to Babasaheb's policies was never seen. Though Periyar was a little assertive in the matter of social justice, Babu Jagjivan Ram was different from today's Dalit leaders. He was a strong opponent of leading Dalits to violence and separatism under the influence of the Left, unlike many Dalit leaders of today.

Dr. Ram Manohar Lohia, who envisioned a socialist India, had a dream for the backward, downtrodden, poor, deprived society of India, but his so-called disciples – Mulayam Singh Yadav and Lalu Prasad Yadav sought power on the strength of Yadav-Muslim alliance and therefore became strong opponents of Dalits.

On the basis of the 2011 Census of the country, if seen, 16.6 per cent, that is, 20.14 crore population of the country is Dalit, but the leaders who are supposed to lead this Dalit population, themselves do not know what they have to do for the development of Dalits. They are trying to mislead the Dalits under the guise of a few abbots of power. These abbots are engaged in toppling the government of Prime Minister Narendra Modi in the name of the Dalit-Muslim alliance, while the country has formed a clear majority government with a thumping majority to put an end to the coalition politics that lasted for almost three decades. This government is working tirelessly with positive thinking for the development of Dalits and Adivasis. After all, our Dalit leaders today raise slogans of 'Jai Bhim' in the name of Babasaheb, but in the name of Dalit empowerment, they are working completely against the path shown by Dr. Ambedkar. By doing this, they may themselves become an MP or MLA from this unusual Dalit-Muslim-Leftist alliance, but the damage and danger that they are exposing the Dalit society to will not be compensated in the coming years. Through CAA, the government wants to give a dignified life to the minority Hindus, mostly Dalits, by bringing them back into the Hindu fold, as they are living a neglected life in Pakistan and Bangladesh, but our Dalit leaders are opposing it under the enticement of Leftists and Muslim separatists. Surely Babasaheb would have suffered immense pain had he been alive today.

□

Ambedkar's Perspective on Integral Humanism

It is often said that there were differences in the economic and social policies of Jana Sangh (currently BJP) and Babasaheb, but this was never the case. Dr. Ambedkar wanted to bring the Dalits and the downtrodden of the society, who had been exploited for centuries, into the mainstream of the nation. That is why he thought it better to fight for the welfare of Dalit society in India. Henceforth he gave up on his luxurious life despite of acquiring higher education abroad. The Bharatiya Janata Party also follows the idea of integral humanism as its fundamental basis, inspired by its ideal leader, Pt. Deendayal Upadhyay.

Pt. Upadhyay saw the individual and society as a whole. Therefore, for the complete development of the individual, not only the fulfilment of physical and economic needs are required but his spiritual and intellectual development too was considered necessary by him. He believed that along with alleviating the economic hunger of the society, its cultural, spiritual and intellectual hunger had to be addressed. In order to keep the society healthy in all respect, emphasis was given to providing a practical form to *dharma* (moral duties), *artha* (wealth), *kama* (desire or satisfaction), and *moksha* (salvation) in the society. With regard to picturing a completely healthy society, *antyodaya* was a requisite. *Antyodaya* means that even the person standing at the end of the row can get his fair share of profits. Therefore for establishing *antyodaya* he talked about *arthyayam* in the society, that is, the distribution system should be such, which can benefit the last person. Only then all-around development of the human being is possible and this is the basic concept of integralism.

Pt. Deendayal Upadhyay presented this concept in the Gwalior session of Jana Sangh on 10th August, 1964, and taking inspiration from it, the foremost goal of the party was decided in the year 1965 under the document titled, *Principle and Policy*. According to this, the focal point of our entire system should be humans and this remains our main objective even today. Describing the purpose of the establishment of Bharatiya Jana Sangh as *antyodaya*, Pt. Deendayal Upadhyay said, "The knowledge of the world is our treasure, the experience of mankind is our property. India is our amphitheatre and the vast majority of people of India are not only the characters of this theatre, but they are also the spectators, for whose enjoyment and self-pleasure we have to play the roles of all. We are not only watchers but also seekers of world progress. Therefore, while on the one hand, our eyes should be on the achievements of the world, on the other hand, we should identify the basic nature and talent of the nation and determine the future development course according to our traditions and situations. The elimination of ignorance, want and injustice and the beginning of a strong, prosperous and happy national life depends upon voluntary labour and cooperation of all. This great work requires new leadership in every sphere of the nation's life. Bharatiya Jana Sangh was born to fulfil this expectation. The objective of the Bharatiya Jana Sangh is to make India a political, social and economic democracy on the basis of its culture and dignity, in which the individuals get equal opportunities and freedom, which makes India strong and prosperous, making it a progressive, modern and aware nation, which can successfully face the attacks of others and make a proper impact in the League of Nations for the establishment of world peace."

Babasaheb Dr. Ambedkar also tried to empower the Dalits and the deprived society in his own way. He emphasised social reforms rather than politics and opposed Untouchability. Babasaheb used to insist that before the advent of the *Manusmriti* era, the Shudras were equal partners in the development of society and after that, with the entry of Muslim rulers in the medieval period, especially after the establishment of the Slave dynasty, the exploitation of Hindus began. The Hindus had to pay a tax called *jaziya* to protect themselves and to avoid conversion. The Hindus who refused to pay the *jaziya* tax were forced to convert to Islam, were subjected to severe torture, had to do manual scavenging and were compelled to eat dead animals and were abhorred.

"The Hindu society also suffered a moral decline at the same time. The brave Brahmins and Kshatriyas, who had to scavenge when they retaliated, were declared Untouchables by other Hindus. When Islam came to India, the Dalits were only one per cent at that time; their number increased to 14 per cent. It is clear that today's downtrodden class is the same, whose brave ancestors endured torture, but did not accept Islam, even though they were excommunicated from society. We should pay homage to those who, while struggling, kept the saffron flag high and did not allow it to bow down, even though at a personal level they had to pay a great price for it" (Dr. Subramanian Swamy: *Hindutva and National Renaissance*).

In the same book, Dr. Swami further writes: "The birth-based social structure is not according to any theology. Birth is not the basis of *varna* in Hindu texts. It is a selected alternative form based on *karma*, which a person can choose according to himself. The present form of the *varna* system is non-Hindu. For the sake of universal Hindu unity, it is preferable to discard this burden at the earliest in the interest of the nation."

Similarly, opposing casteism, while speaking at the convocation at Gurukul Kangri in the year 1952, Hindu thinker and scholar and founder of Jana Sangh, Dr. Syama Prasad Mookerjee said, "We are not unhappy that the British Raj opened the doors of education to Indians. We are sad about the fact that this education is going to suppress our own great culture, heritage and knowledge. We should inculcate pride in the hearts of young Indian students about our national traditions and heritage. We should awaken such consciousness that they learn to live above caste and community" (Dr. Subramanian Swamy: *Hindutva and National Renaissance*).

Mahant Adityanathji of Goraksha Peethadheesh has also suggested paving the way for collective integration by dissolving the practice of Untouchability and high and low for a national renaissance. In his words, "Hindutva's national renaissance requires an all-inclusive movement, whose goal is to remove the evils of Untouchability, casteism, dowry and class discrimination. By dissolving the disruptive policy of Untouchability, high and low, and discrimination on the basis of birth in the same society, paving the way for social integration, the vast Hindu society has to be holistic and strengthened by providing a harmonious life" (*Hindutva ek Jeevanshaili*, Prabhat Prakashan).

According to Babasaheb's desires and aspiration, *antyodaya* has been envisaged in 'Integral Humanism', whose goal is to establish such a society above the spirit of caste and sect and in which everyone has equal opportunities and no one is deprived of these opportunities on the basis of caste or sect. This is the goal of *antyodaya* BJP. Pt. Deendayal Upadhyay became the leader of the ideological side of this theory and Atal Bihari Vajpayee did the work of highlighting his ideological aspect while Prime Minister Narendra Modi is executing the task of giving it a concrete shape.

There are some socialists in the country, who do politics in the name of Dr. Ram Manohar Lohia, Acharya Narendra Dev, Lok Nayak Jayaprakash Narayan and Karpoori Thakur, but when it comes to the development of the Dalits and the downtrodden, they create hurdles. In the year 2013, when the debate on the Scheduled Castes and Scheduled Tribes Reservation Bill was going on in the Parliament, Samajwadi Party leader Mulayam Singh Yadav, along with his entire supporters, opposed this bill on the ground that if this bill is passed, the efficiency of administration will be affected and the country will not be able to get qualified officers. How did the hon'ble Mulayam Singh forget that the castes, which have started considering themselves extremely efficient, were not given a post higher than that of an Office Superintendent and a Deputy Superintendent of Police in the time of the British? Today there are about 40 people in his family as MP, MLA, block presidents, etc., so what test of proficiency has he passed? They have only misled people in the name of the Yadav and Muslim alliance.

In any event, the Dalits and the downtrodden of the country have proficiently fulfilled the responsibilities assigned to them. As the chairman of the Drafting Committee of the constitution, Dr. Ambedkar created a constitution that is considered to be one of the best constitutions in the world. During the *Bhakti* period, when many evils were enrooted in society, Dalit saint Ravidas gave a new direction to society. Not only this, Maharishi Valmiki and Veda Vyasa produced two great texts for Hindus – the *Ramayana* and the *Mahabharata*. Both of them were born and belonged to the Shudra caste. When democracy was established in Independent India, Babu Jagjivan Ram, a Dalit, was among the most successful ministers of India. As the Agriculture Minister of India, he brought in the 'Green Revolution', which made India self-reliant in the matter of food production. Bangladesh's conquest also took place during his tenure as Defence Minister. Therefore, there is a need to drop the prejudice that the efficiency of administration will be affected by the participation of Dalits. The need of the hour is to include the Dalits and the downtrodden in the mainstream of the nation and this is the philosophy of 'Integral Humanism'. The goal of 'Integral Humanism' is the establishment of such a society. Religion is our basic pursuit. Its goal is the welfare of all and the progress of body-mind-intellect-spirit – that is, *antyodaya* is its essence.

□

Babasaheb Wanted Complete Transfer of Population

Dr. Krishna Gopal, an eminent scholar and Sah Sarkaryavah of Rashtriya Swayamsevak Sangh, has written in his book, *Babasaheb: Vyaktitva aur Vichaar*, that the partition of the country was a tragic event. There was horrific massacre all over the country. Lakhs of people were killed, while millions were severely injured. Babasaheb Ambedkar was deeply saddened to see this. He wrote in a letter to his friend Kamalakant Chitre: "It cannot be called a riot; it would be fair to call it an armed rebellion. A large number of people were killed and equally injured. It is very terrible for a city like Delhi. Life in Delhi has come to a standstill for many days." Dr. Ambedkar had proposed complete population transfer with the partition of the country. He said that the Muslim and Hindu populations should go to their respective countries, so that civil war and horrific genocide could be avoided.

When the British decided to partition India on communal lines, Dr. Ambedkar very well knew that Muslims would never live peacefully with Hindus in a non-Muslim State. On the one hand, the leaders of Congress, Left parties and Muslim organisations supported the devious policy of the British to form Pakistan, while on the other hand, nationalist parties and organisations, including the Hindu Mahasabha and Rashtriya

Swayamsevak Sangh were constantly opposed to partition. Among the non-Muslim leaders, Dr. Ambedkar was probably the first person to accept the demand of Pakistan in 1940 itself. He asserted that it was no longer possible for the two communities to live in peace within a nation and therefore supported the idea of a complete population swap. He said that he understood the partition between "Muslim India and non-Muslim India better, as it is the surest and safest way to provide security to both communities. It is more secure than other available alternatives, i.e. Muslims across the country should be allowed to go to Pakistan. A mandatory plan should be made to send and bring the Hindus living there to India."

Speaking on 'Thoughts on Pakistan' at Bombay, in February 1942, Dr. Ambedkar said that there was no use in arguing with those who did not want to discuss Pakistan. "If the creation of Pakistan seems to them to be an injustice, then the creation of Pakistan will be terrible for them. It would be a grave mistake to ask people to forget history because history forgetters cannot create history. It would be wise to make the army monogamous and patriotic by freeing the Indian Army from the influence of Muslims. We will protect our motherland ourselves."

Dr. Ambedkar had also prepared a detailed action plan for the complete transfer of population in the event of partition and this he had put before everyone in the year 1940 through his book, *Pakistan and Partition of India*. Dr. Ambedkar's plan was that after the Ottoman Empire, the way population was transferred between Greece, Turkey and Bulgaria, in the same way, it could be possible in India as well. In his plan, he had also put forward a plan of action to exchange the rights of property, pension, etc., which the Congress rejected because the Congress leaders were wandering in false fantasies of a Hindu-Muslim alliance. The well-known author Koenraad Elst, in his book,

Indigenous India (pp. 401-02) acknowledged the differences between the Congress's leadership and Ambedkar's leadership while describing the mentality of the Congress. Dr. Ambedkar put forth the form of a clean and permanent settlement, but Mahatma Gandhi and Pandit Jawaharlal Nehru refused to give up on the destructive daydream of Hindu-Muslim unity. Even after fully accepting the two-nation theory, the theory of total transfer of population was completely rejected.

Dr. Ambedkar had, at various points in time, said that the people will be completely trapped in Pakistan after the formation of Pakistan. Therefore, there should be a system to remove them safely before partition. Despite all the efforts, Dr. Ambedkar's plan and proposal were not accepted and after the partition in 1947, a large number of the Hindu population, other than the Scheduled Castes, stayed behind in Pakistan. But after a few days, the true face of Hindu-Muslim unity started appearing in front of the people. The life of the Hindus living there turned from bad to worse due to unnecessary pressures and beatings on a daily basis in pursuit to convert the Hindus to Muslims. Lakhs of Hindus, who protested, were killed and their properties were confiscated. At the time of partition, due to a lack of complete exchange of population, more than half of the Muslims stayed behind in India and whose number has now increased to more than 150 million, while the population of Hindus living in Pakistan has decreased from one crore to just a few thousand.

Babasaheb used to argue behind his theory of population transfer that because of the aggressive nature of the Muslims, they proceed towards hooliganism to take advantage of the weakness of the Hindu society. The proof of this is found in the fact that even in Independent India, Waris Pathan, the heir to Owaisi's party, openly declares on the stage that 15 crores of Muslims will prevail over 100 crore Hindus. Babasaheb wrote and said a lot about the regressive and anti-national tendencies of Muslims. He clearly believed that as long as Muslims continued to consider themselves Muslims, they cannot be assimilated into India. Dr. Ambedkar used to repeat time and again that Muslims cannot be amalgamated with the Hindus. They are such foreign elements that it would be appropriate to throw them out of the body of the nation. It was at this point that he spoke of the complete migration of the population (Dr. Krishna Gopal: *Babasaheb: Vyaktitva aur Vichaar*, p. 226). He knew very well that it is a difficult task to move such a large population from one place to another, but he believed that if it was kept optional, then that would lead to the formation of Pakistan and the problem would still remain unsolved. It would remain so because the leaders of the Muslim League had started to say that even in the event of the formation of Pakistan, not all the Muslims of the country would be required to move to Pakistan.

Dr. Ambedkar suggested that a commission should be formed for this transfer of population as it would help in relocating people by preparing detailed information about all the movable and immovable property, pensions, jobs, etc. He had in detail mentioned the plan he had prepared regarding relocation, in his book, *Pakistan or Partition of India*. Dr. Ambedkar said that only a complete exchange of population can make India a nation. Unless this is done, the creation of Pakistan will not solve the problem of minorities and the majority in the country. Minority Hindus in Pakistan will continue to live a life of disgrace and poor minority Muslims in India will continue to be misled by the leaders doing politics over Muslims' and Dalits' unity and hatred will find place in the politics of the country. But unfortunately, at that time, Mahatma Gandhi, Nehru and other Congress leaders did not listen to Babasaheb Ambedkar and remained in the trap of secularism, as mute witnesses to the massacre of lakhs of people at the time of partition of the country.

After seven decades of Independence, when the BJP leadership took a positive initiative through CAA to give a life of honour to the persecuted minority Hindus in Pakistan, then again Shaheen Bagh had to be closed due to protests sponsored by Congress and Left parties. Nobody can tell for how long these parties will continue to resort to such tactics in desperation at being deprived of power! Although Dr. Ambedkar did not favour the partition of the country, the circumstances in the country had turned violent. Also, Muhammad Ali Jinnah had found a leader in the form of Jogendra Nath Mandal, who was trapped in the illusion of a pseudo-Dalit-Muslim alliance and additionally wasn't even ready to listen to any argument against it. His insistence ultimately resulted in the creation of Pakistan which was witness to bloodshed of the Dalit society.

In 1945, Babasaheb Dr. Ambedkar wrote, in his book, *Thoughts on Pakistan*, "Muslims are opposed to social reforms. The brotherhood that Islam talks about is not the brotherhood of all human beings in the world; it is only the brotherhood of Muslims with Muslims. For non-Muslims, there is only hatred and enmity, plus Islam does not allow any Muslim to be loyal to a non-Muslim." Dr. Ambedkar further wrote, "In such a situation, it is better to allow Pakistan to be formed because it is difficult for non-Muslims to live a life of dignity and equality in a Muslim-majority area."

□

Integration of Dalits into the Mainstream

Mahatma Gandhi wrote of Congress leaders' indifference towards Dalits: "There is no need to elaborate on the need to wash away the stigma and curse of Untouchability that clings to Hinduism in today's time. The Congressmen have done a lot in this direction, but I have to say with regret that most of the Congressmen have considered the removal of Untouchability as a political necessity, instead of considering it necessary for the existence of Hinduism itself. If the Congressmen take up this work, understanding that there is significance in it, by doing this they will be able to change the heart of their religious brothers who are called Sanatanis and can have a manifold effect on them" (Ramshankar Agnihotri: *Bharat Ratna Dr. Ambedkar*, 1994). Basically, there is no difference between Mahatma Gandhi's and Dr. Ambedkar's answers to the Dalit question, yet there is definitely a dissimilarity in the way of making their dreams a reality. The result of Mahatma Gandhi's efforts was that the Congress emerged as a party of Dalits all over India and the Dalits also gained confidence in the Congress. Till the 1978 elections, Dalits and Muslims remained the majority in the vote bank politics of the Congress; its political expression was in the form of Babu Jagjivan Ram, but after the Emergency, when Babu Jagjivan Ram left the Congress and formed Congress for Democracy, this trust was shattered. Subsequently, Kanshi Ram drew this vote away from the Congress permanently. The Congress did not consider Babasaheb as a Dalit leader, whereas Babasaheb was the leading messenger of Dalit upliftment and wanted to bring the Dalit society into the mainstream of the nation.

The evils of society block the pace of development of a society. The evils prevalent in Hinduism for centuries had blocked the movement of Dalit society. At this time, the Dalit society needed a social reformer, who could generate potential in them and could recognise his own potential so that the society could move forward by taking inspiration from that person's work. In the context of the Dalit society of India, such a person was Babasaheb Ambedkar. From slave India to Independent India, Dr. Ambedkar devoted his life completely to the welfare of the Dalit and downtrodden section of the society.

Even before him, social reformers like Jyotiba Phule, Chhatrapati Shahuji Maharaj, Karmaveer Shinde, Tribhuvan, etc. wanted social change. In such a situation, when Babasaheb Ambedkar emerged on the social scene, he undertook the overall change of social conditions. He believed that the poison of caste discrimination and Untouchability had divided society and made the nation weak and shabby. On one hand, the believers of Sanatan Dharma used to talk about *vasudaiva kutumbakam*, at the same time, in this holy land, his followers disregarded the all-pervading principle of 'soul-*parmatma*' propounded by them by giving rise to the reprehensible caste-discrimination system, like high-low and Untouchability with human beings. Due to this flawed system of society, crores of Dalits have led a humiliating and hellish life for hundreds of years. Babasaheb was of the firm opinion that this distinction had to be removed and people have to accept that the people of the Scheduled Castes are as faithful to Hindutva as the other Hindus. Therefore, discrimination on the basis of caste should end (Dr. Bhimrao Ambedkar: *Who were Shudras*). Saying this, he did not sit still but took the path of struggle against the inequality prevailing in society. He wanted that all the rights enjoyed by the Hindus should be given to the marginalised and deprived section of the society.

Dr. Ambedkar believed in social change and in his opinion, it would not be right to stop social change for the sake of speeding up the political change, rather, social reform should be done as a precursor to political change; whereas, Congress focused on political issues instead of aiming at social change.

Tilak, Gandhi, Patel, Nehru, Malviya and all the other leaders did not pay attention to the social evils prevailing at that time; rather, all of them had one thing in their mind– first Independence should be achieved, and after that, the fight against social evils should be fought. But Dr. Ambedkar disagreed with this and prioritised social reform over political reform. This was the reason why Dr. Ambedkar engaged in the work of social reform without waiting for political change. At the time when his movement started on the Indian horizon, Hindu society was already caught in the web of conservatism, traditionalism, casteism, Untouchability, feudalism and many more such evil practices (Dr. Krishna Gopal: *Babasaheb: Vyaktitva aur Vichaar*, p. 41). Dr. Ambedkar wanted to abandon the rigid ancient religious orthodox texts. He wished that these orthodox rules should be replaced by a religion based on principles. Now, this does not mean that he was not a supporter of Independent India, but he wanted to ensure the development of the deprived society and include it in the mainstream of the nation.

Due to family values, the spirit of Hindutva was filled with a sense of firmness in Dr. Ambedkar's mind. From student life till 1930, we see him as a strong Hindu fighting against the customs and evils prevalent in Hindu society. Till 1935, he used to begin by writing 'Jai Bhavani' in all the letters he had written. Through temple entrance and permission to fill water on public ponds, wells, etc., he wanted reforms and consolidation within the Hindu society. He hoped that by writings, speeches and agitations, if needed, the mentality of the upper caste society would be affected and they would definitely have a change of heart.

Dr. Ambedkar believed that there should be no discrimination on the basis of caste within the Hindu society and therefore he gathered people in opposition to it and started preparing for peaceful movements. He, however, never pushed Dalits into the fire of violence like today's leaders, such as Chandrashekhar (Ravana), Kancha Ilaiah, etc. do; his movement was always peaceful.

Through movements like Mahad *satyagraha*, Nashik temple *satyagraha* and Dadar's Ganeshotsav, Dr. Ambedkar gave all the rights to the Dalits as the Dalit and deprived society was expecting from this great social reformer. As a consequence of the constant struggle of Dr. Ambedkar and other social reformers, a new era of social change commenced. Due to this change taking place in society, the nature of somc positive evolutions started appearing in the society. A positive shift in the society was experienced - contrary to Babasaheb being forced to study, sitting in the verandah outside the classroom during his primary education, now the children of Dalits could go to schools and colleges. Due to the basis of old conservative ideas and malpractices, there was a change in the thoughts and behaviour of the people and the spread of education, access to the means of transport and the feeling of nationalism were now visible in the society. In the eyes of Dr. Ambedkar, national interest was paramount and that is why after completing higher education in economics at London, he left a good and comfortable life and came to India because he loved his nation and society immensely.

In his view, national interest was supreme and which is why he did not agree with the Muslim disintegrators because the Muslim leaders always denied the possibility of co-existence with the Hindus. Today, some people talk about Dalit and Muslim alliance in their personal selfishness, whereas the reality is that Muslims can never support Dalits. If this was not the case, then in the year 2017, Mayawati's Dalit-Muslim alliance formula in the Assembly elections would not have failed and instead of voting for Mayawati's party, the Muslims voted for Mulayam Singh Yadav. Aware of the real situation, Dr. Ambedkar did not support any kind of alliance for political selfishness. The views expressed in his book, *My Thoughts on Pakistan* reveal the reality of this fact.

It is extremely unfortunate that people see him merely as a Dalit leader. It is true that he fought continuously for the Dalit society, but in reality, he cared for the society as a whole. He was a staunch nationalist and had a broad outlook. He was devoted to the interests of the Dalit society, but he considered the development of the entire society as the basis for progress of the nation. He was a bitter critic of the upper castes on the question of the caste system, but he never accepted the demand for expelling the upper castes who displayed a far-sighted vision in their movements. He blamed the Brahmins for the age-old caste system, but never hated them; he always respected the learned Brahmins. He knew that service or kindness would not change the lives of the people. For this, the self-respect of Dalits would have to be strengthened. He did not want to lead the Dalits and downtrodden to violent struggles like today's Dalit leaders do. His main objective was that the Dalits should become educated and self-reliant and join the mainstream of the nation. His entire personality is exemplary as it stands like a steadfast and unshakable lighthouse despite the brutal blows of the times.

□

Ambedkar's Views on Inclusion in Scheduled Caste List to Dalits who have Converted to other Religions

Under the leadership of Dr. Manmohan Singh, the UPA government, formed in the year 2004, continued to make efforts to see that Dalits who had become Christians or Muslims through conversion should be proved to be Dalits and included in the Scheduled Castes. The purpose was not Dalit upliftment but an attempt to appeasement, because the UPA government was indirectly being run by Mrs. Sonia Gandhi who wanted to increase the number of Christians and Muslims in India. Therefore, she wanted to introduce a system wherein, even after conversion, the reservation facility given to the Dalit as a Scheduled Caste would not end. It had been seen that in spite of lakhs of temptations given by Christian missionaries and Muslim organisations, many Dalits did not convert because they did not want to lose their identity.

It is absolutely necessary to know what Babasaheb Dr. Ambedkar's views were regarding the converts because the Congress and its supporters often allege that the BJP obstructs the development of Dalits by opposing reservation for these converted Dalits. In 2004, when this resolution was brought in by the Congress, there was strong opposition by the BJP

Shri Ram Nath Kovind, then the National President of BJP (S.C. Morcha) and the former President of the country. When the Round Table Conference, held in 1930, was a complete failure, Dr. Ambedkar accused the British Government of neglecting the upliftment of the Depressed Classes and this provided a new twist to the Dalit movement. In the same Round Table Conference, Babasaheb put forth the demand for separate electorates for Dalits, opposing which, Mahatma Gandhi sat on a hunger strike. As a result of it, an agreement was signed between Gandhi and Ambedkar on 24th September to stop the demand for separate electorates. This marked the signing of the historic Poona Pact. The same agreement proceeded in the form of a special arrangement (reservation) for the empowerment of Dalit society after the first caste Census held in 1931 for the upliftment of Dalits. In 1935, after identifying 429 Hindu castes, a schedule was prepared by the British Government and in 1936, recognising them as Scheduled Castes, reservation was recommended for them.

When the construction of the list of Scheduled Castes was going on, a strong effort was made to include the converted Muslims in it, but the British Government rejected this demand saying that there was a belief in the world that Christians and Islam believed society to be casteless and so how could Christians and Muslims who had become converts be included in the list of Scheduled Castes? If this happened, then the topic of the upliftment of Dalits through Scheduled Castes would become meaningless. Dr. Ambedkar welcomed this idea of the British and thanked them.

When the country became Independent in 1947 and the responsibility of making the constitution was entrusted to Dr. Ambedkar, many forces interested in depriving the Dalits of their rights became active again. In this way, the real ordeal of Babasaheb started. He had to face and answer the questions in favour and against reservation for Scheduled Castes while pursuing the task of writing the constitution. He stood up to hundreds of questions from converted Christians and Muslims and gave a befitting reply to their unreasonable arguments. Ultimately, Dr. Ambedkar vehemently rejected the demand for the inclusion of converted Muslims and Christians in the Scheduled Caste category. This action of Ambedkar clearly portrayed his commitment to the upliftment of the Dalit society. He believed that this had long been a demand sponsored by Christian missionaries. The reason behind this demand was nothing but the promotion of conversion. Dr. Ambedkar believed that the Scheduled Castes could not be tempted to give up their religious faith on being lured by temptations.

For this reason, when he decided to leave Hinduism on getting fed up with the evils of the Hindu society, he faced various temptations to become a Christian or a Muslim, but he rejected all of them. He clarified that the fraternity of Christians and Muslims was limited only to their followers and their brotherhood with other non-Muslims and non-Christians was insubstantial.

In fact, Ambedkar was a reformist Hindu and this was the reason that he left Hinduism and adopted Buddhism, which flourished at one time in India. Before leaving Hinduism, he had said on an open platform, "Contractors of Hinduism, reform yourself otherwise we will renounce Hinduism along with lakhs of Dalits." Just a month and twenty-three days before his death, he adopted Buddhism, arguing that "we have changed the room, not the house"; that is, he adopted the same religion in which Hindu culture resides. Dr. Ambedkar made it clear that if the Dalit society had to leave Hinduism and refuse to be trapped into Christianity or Islam, then it should adopt Buddhism (Dr. Krishna Gopal: *Babasaheb: Vyaktitva aur Vichaar*, p. 253).

Ambedkar completely opposed the inclusion of converted Christians and Muslims in the list of Scheduled Castes. He stood firm on the 429 castes, which were included in the list of Scheduled Castes in 1936, and parties like SP-BSP wanted to include 17 more OBC castes from the OBC list into the scheduled list to increase their vote bank.

The author is of the view that if these parties really had the welfare of these backward castes in mind, then in the 27 per cent reservation of OBC, some percentage should have been reserved for them because, to include them in the scheduled list, was tantamount to betrayal of the Scheduled Caste.

In 2004, the Congress-run UPA government made every effort to include the converted Christians and Muslims in the scheduled list. Although this demand was never included by any of the former Prime Ministers, like Pandit Jawaharlal Nehru, Lal Bahadur Shastri, Indira Gandhi, Morarji Desai, Chaudhary Charan Singh, V.P. Singh, Narasimha Rao, Deve Gowda or Atal Bihari Vajpayee, but the remote-controlled Prime Minister Dr. Manmohan Singh tried to fufil this demand. Rajiv Gandhi first made this effort in 1985, but due to heavy opposition in Gujarat, he had to relinquish his efforts.

In the year 2005, during the tenure of Dr. Manmohan Singh, the National Commission for Religious and Linguistic Minorities was formed and it was headed by Justice Ranganath Mishra. Through this Commission, the social, economic and other conditions of the converted Christians and Muslims were studied. Sardar Buta Singh, the then chairman of the Scheduled Castes Commission, betrayed the Dalits by recommending that they should be included in the Scheduled Castes, while he himself was a very prominent Dalit leader and was the Home Minister in the Rajiv Gandhi government. Perhaps due to his strong desire to return to the mainstream of politics, he had to succumb to the pressure of Sonia Gandhi. Justice Ranganath

Misra, as the chairman of the commission, recommended the inclusion of converted Christians and Muslims in the Scheduled Castes and which the government had to accept, but the then secretary of the commission, Mrs. Asha Das, sent a dissent note on behalf of the commission, clarifying with many points that the converted Christians and converted Muslims cannot be included in the list of Scheduled Castes at any cost. In this regard, it is also necessary to mention that in the year 2004, the Supreme Court of India issued a notice to the Central Government asking for the reason for including the converted Christians and converted Muslims in the Scheduled Caste list. The UPA government went to the Supreme Court and said that the government had no objection. On this answer from the government, the Supreme Court jumped into action and the Ranganath Misra Commission was formed.

In fact, the UPA government had no other motive other than conversion for including the converted Christians and Muslims in the Scheduled Castes. Had they been included in the Scheduled Castes list, then the Depressed Classes would have become Christians by falling prey to the temptations offered by Christian missionaries.

The late Ashok Singhal, Ram Nath Kovind (former President of India), Prime Minister Narendra Modi, Rajnath Singh and Nitin Gadkari played an important role in putting a spoke in the wheels of this conspiracy by Congress. The Uttar Pradesh government later decided to include 17 OBC castes in the Scheduled Castes but this idea was rejected by Thawar Chand Gehlot the Minister of Social Justice and Empowerment in the Parliament. Behind all this, Ambedkar's broad thinking is the basic foundation, which he has been interested in since the time of the Poona Pact.

□

The Icon who Recognised the Genius of Dr. Ambedkar-Chhatrapati Shahuji Maharaj

Today each and every political party is constrained to praise Dr. Ambedkar. Some remember him as the architect of the constitution, some remember him as an economist for establishing the Reserve Bank of India and the Finance Commission in India, while the Bahujan Samaj remembers him as the saviour of the Dalits and downtrodden section of the society. Some Manuwadis remember him as the biggest villain for introducing reservation. Whether the Leftists or the Rightists, everyone remembers Babasaheb though as long as the Congress remained in power, Babasaheb's name was seldom taken. For his invaluable contribution to nation building, constitution-making, Babasaheb was awarded the Bharat Ratna in 1990 after 42 years of the Independence. The same year, his oil painting was installed in the Central Hall of Parliament.

It was in 1920, when Chhatrapati Shahuji Maharaj came to know about the genius of Dr. Ambedkar, he declared in a public meeting, "I think in Ambedkar you have found your liberator. I hope he will break the shackles of your slavery." Remembering the work done by Shahuji Maharaj 50 years before Independence for the Dalits and downtrodden will be a true tribute to Dr. Ambedkar.

Babasaheb himself used to say that it is very important for every community to know its history. Only the nation which remembers its golden history can create the future. There are plenty of descriptions of Lord Rama and Ramrajya in Brahmin culture, but very little is known about Chhatrapati Shahuji Maharaj, the Maharaja of Shramana culture. Any great man is recognised by the work done by him. On 26th June, 1874, Shahuji Maharaj, born in the Kurmi (Patidar) caste of the Shudra *varna*, devoted his life to fulfilling the dreams of Jyotiba Phule and Savitribai Phule to end the caste system and discrimination. The 10-year-old Shahu was declared the heir to the throne in 1884 and when he turned 20, he was crowned king of the princely state of Kolhapur on 2nd July, 1894.

After receiving his early education in Rajkot (Gujarat) at Rajkumar Vidyalaya, Shahuji went in for further education from an English teacher, Stuart Mitford Frageret, at home. Due to the influence of English teachers and English education, scientific thinking developed in him, prompting him to reject obsolete customs, traditions and superstitions. He studied political science, economics, science, and languages as also other important books, including *Letters to an Indian Raja* by Mahatma Phule's friend Narayan Mahadev Parmanand, better known as Mama Parmanand. Shahuji was educated abroad and in June 1902, he received an L.L.D from Cambridge University. He was the first Indian to receive such an honorary degree. In addition to it, he also achieved GCSI, GCVO and MRES.

Shahuji himself was against the caste system. There is an anecdote of October 1902, when Shahuji went to take a bath in the Panchganga river. On seeing him, the *rajpurohit* (royal priest) started reciting *mantras* without taking a bath as Shahuji was a Shudra. Shahuji's *rajpurohit* refused to perform the bathing ceremony of Shahuji and his family members. This painful practice in the caste system hurt Sahuji's mind and brain.

A similar incident occurred when Shahuji Maharaj was prevented from entering the kitchen of Brahmins, simply because he was a Shudra king. Shahuji observed that cats could roam freely in the kitchen, but a Shudra king could not enter the kitchen. He thought that if the Brahmins could behave in such a degrading manner with a king, then what would be the condition of the general public? It was from here that the war against the inhuman caste system began. He began to agitate against the supremacy of Brahmins over the state and society. He tried to bring a social revolution by taking certain steps.

In 1901, Shahuji Maharaj got a Census conducted in Kolhapur and it was discovered that there were 1,03,889 Untouchables in Kolhapur state. The report highlighted not only the plight of the Untouchables but also that of the Other Backward Classes (OBCs). On the basis of this Census report, he issued an ordinance on 26 July 1902 that 50 per cent reservation would be provided for backward classes in education and government jobs of the princely state of Kolhapur. That is why he is known as the 'father of reservation'. In 1894, when Shahuji Maharaj took over the reins of the state, out of a total of 71 posts in the general administration of Kolhapur, 60 officers were Brahmin. Similarly, out of 500 posts for clerks, only 10 were given to non-Brahmins. In 1912, out of 95 posts, Shahuji got the number of Brahmin officers reduced to 35 due to 50 per cent reservation for backward castes. He also realised that social change was meaningless without the spread of education. So he made every effort to make modern education available to the backward classes.

Subsequently, in 1912, he made primary education compulsory. Failure in propagation of education promped him to pass an ordinance in 1913. This led to schools being opened in every village with a population of 500 to 1,000 and for this, he announced a grant of one lakh rupees from the government treasury. He also laid special emphasis on the education of girls. He was the first king in the history of India, who made primary education compulsory and free on 25th July, 1917. He opened a free hostel in 1920. An Untouchable student named Bhaskar Vithoji Jadhav passed with first division in Class X and later was appointed as a probationary assistant in government service. This riledthe Brahmins who began to dub Shahuji the 'king of *dhors* (animals)'. He passed various ordinances related to Untouchability between 1918 and 1919, in which provisions were made for providing schools, hostels, scholarships and other facilities to the Untouchables interested in modern education. On 30th September, 1919, he opened the doors of all public schools to the Untouchables and on 22nd August, 1919, he issued an ordinance warning the state officials against the practice of discrimination against Untouchables.

In 1919, Shahuji issued an order, according to which any person from the Untouchable society could seek treatment as hospitals. He was of the view that economic development and progress of India depended on abolition of the caste system. He also abolished the system of priests in villages. Along with this he also issued orders for the appointment of Marathas (backward-caste priests). In 1920, he opened schools for worship and training of priests.

The Brahmins were strongly opposed to these actions of Shahuji and turned to Bal Gangadhar Tilak for help. Tilak, in an address to the public, "*Teli-tamboli kunbhatto* (Kurmi)' has to go to Parliament to plow, do tailors have to go to Parliament to sew clothes?" At this, Shahuji not only condemned these words of Tilak, but also targeted the Congress which had remained silent over it. What is more, he even rejected Gopal Krishna Gokhale's invitation to join the Congress. For him, Bhimrao Ambedkar was the only hope for his war against the caste system, so in 1920, he declared openly, "I think you have found your liberator in Ambedkar. I hope they will break the shackles of your slavery."

Shahuji, who was awarded the title of 'Rajarshi' at the 13th National Conference of the All India Kurmi Mahasabha held at Kanpur on 9th-21st April, 1919, buthe died on 6th May, 1922, at the young age of only 48. Well-known biographer Dhananjay Keer has written about Shahuji, "Chhatrapati's patriotism is the development of his heart and the development of human service was ingrained in him. Many good kings and leaders have come and gone in India and royal palaces of the emperors have been erased from the map, but only the names of the kings have remained immortal in history. Despite being a mass leader, it is rare to have a royal sage like Shahuji Chhatrapati, who rose on the wave of the people's ocean and shone in royal glory."

□

Hindutva and 'Sarva Dharma Sambhava' as Soul of the Constitution

Recently we saw communal and separatist forces opposing the Citizen Amendment Act and NRC (National Register of Citizens) and accusing Prime Minister Narendra Modi and Home Minister Amit Shah of making India a Hindu *rashtra*. This baseless allegation reflects their policy of communalism and Muslim appeasement. The constitution given to the country by Babasaheb Ambedkar as chairman of the Drafting Committee has Hindutva and *sarvapantha sambhava* as its soul. This fact has been presented by Hindutva thinker Dr. Subramanian Swamy in his book, *Hindutva and National Renaissance*. The structure of our constitution is completely in line with the Hindu tradition. There are several similarities between the two. In ancient times India was made up of *janapadas* and rulers, but it was unitary in nature. The concept of the *chakravarti* emperor, propounded by Chanakya, was that of a power that would become the sole centre of authority in the event of emergency and war, whereas in the ordinary course, the officials were the regional kshatraps. Article 356 of the Constitution of India basically talks about the same.

The Constitution of India, despite being unitary, uses

a federal form to fulfil the regional aspirations, while the tribunals and courts are governed by national interests. In such a situation, the constitution prepared by Dr. Ambedkar is a part of the Hindu tradition and shows continuity. It would, therefore, be relevant to discuss how the present Constitution of India can be integrated with the Hindutva traditions. The impact of Hindutva and Hindu nature on the constitutional and administrative units of Indian states is also clearly visible.

The influence of Hindutva can also be seen in the Parliament of India, which is an important symbol of the Indian democratic system and which is the site of debate on national policy making, where the future of the country is decided. In the Parliament, the words inscribed just above the bench of the Speaker of the Lok Sabha are '*dharma chakra pravartaneeya*'. It is accepted by all that the word *dharma* refers to the Hindu culture. Just as the rulers of ancient India considered religion as the basis of their system of governance, in the same way, the managers of the politics of India accept the same fundamental sentiment and have placed the wheel of religion in the national flag as well.

The message of Hindutva manifests itself in many forms in the Parliament of India:

1. The words inscribed on the entrance 1 of the Parliament are:

लोक द्वारमपात्राणु पश्येम त्वां वयं वेरा।

Lok dwarampatranu pashyem tvaam vyam vera.

(*Chandogya*, 2/24/8)

2. Marked on the entrance of the Central Hall is:

अयं निजः परोवति गणना लघुचेतसाम,
उदारचरितानां तु वसुधैव कुटुम्बकम्।

Ayam nijah parovti gadna laghuchetsaam,
udaarcharitanaam tu vasudhaiva kutumbakam.

(*Panchatantra* 5/38)

It means that only a petty person considers things to be mine and yours, while the whole world is one family of those with a generous character.

3. It is written on the door near lift number 1:

न सा समायत्र न सन्ति वृद्धा
वृद्धाह ना तो यो न व दन्ति धर्मम्
धर्मः स नो यत्र न सत्यमस्ति
सत्य न तचच्छलभ म्यूपैति।

Na sa samayatra na santi vraddha
vraddhah na to yo na va danti dharmam.
Dharmaha sa no yatra na satyamasti
satya na tachhalabh mayupaiti.

(*Mahabharata* 5/35/58)

This means:
It is not a meeting in which there is no old age.
They are not old, who do not speak according to religion.
Where there is no truth, there is no religion.
That which is deceit is not true.

4. The mural of the dome adjacent to lift number 2 is as follows:

सभा वा न प्रवेष्टव्या, वक्तव्यं वा सामज्जसम
अव्रवन विषुवन वा पि नरो भवति किल्विषी।

Sabha va na praveshtavya, vaktavyam va samajjasam,
avvravan vishuvan va pi naro bhavati kilivishi.

(Manu 8/13)

This means that a person should either not enter the assembly at all or if he does so, he should speak according to religion because the one who does not speak or the one who speaks untruth, both are equally guilty of sin.

The said aphorisms, which are inscribed on the walls and domes of the Parliament House, are all reminders of the values that have been prevalent in the beliefs of the leaders of Indian democracy and parliamentary tradition. The original *mantras* in the articles are all taken from Hindu tradition. If we look at the ideals of the central spirit adopted by various institutions of India, then this notion becomes more solid:

1.	Indian Government	*Satyamev Jayate*
2.	Lok Sabha	*Dharma Chakra Pravartaneeya*
3.	The Supreme Court	*Yato Dharmastato Jaya*
4.	All India Radio	*Bhaujan Hitay*
5.	Doordarshan	*Satyam Shivam Sundaram*
6.	Indian Army	*Seva Asmakam Dharma*
7.	Indian Navy	*Shan No Varuna*
8.	Indian Air Force	*abha Sparsham Deeptam*
9.	Life Insurance Corporation of India	*Yogkshemam Vahamayaham*
10.	Delhi University	*Nishtha Dhrati Satyam*

These ideals are ideals in the world of Hindus. As they do not indicate any religious belief, therefore no rituals were invoked in them. These are just the values of civilisation, whose acceptance is deeply humanistic and a commitment to living the right way. These are great qualities which can be considered relevant for the democratic-political future of modern India. The constitution and politics of India emphasise this custom and way of Hindu life, the ancient value system and Hindutva. Similarly, the interpretation of the country's higher judiciary, Hindu customs, or Hindutva has been the socio-cultural basis of ancient India for centuries, and is not a mere legal interpretation. These are fundamentally an acknowledgment of the cultural, ideological and political norms that give the people and regions of India their defining identity. The constitution drafted by Dr. Ambedkar, our Parliament, our supreme judiciary and the vital organs of the state clearly believe that the age-old heritage of Hindu ideals and civilisation will be the ultimate source of inspiration to shape the fate of Independent India.

In a bold decision, the NDA government abolished Article 370 a few years ago. This law gives special status to the state of Jammu & Kashmir. This was a unique provision as it talked of two legislations and two constitutions in the inner region of India and has changed the religious structure of the land from where the Kashmiri Pandits were driven away.

In this regard, it is necessary to refer to Articles 29 and 30 of the Constitution. Article 29 says: 'Protection of interests of minorities, any section of the citizens residing in the territory of India or any part thereof having a distinct language, script or culture of its own shall have the right to conserve the same.' This facility was given because the country was partitioned on communal lines in 1947 and to serve the purpose of providing security to the minorities who did not want to go to Pakistan from India. But a few years ago, the Supreme Court commented on the case that Uniform Civil Code of conduct is necessary for the country because different laws of different religions violate the rights of women in the matter of marriage, divorce, etc.

The constitutional provision for maintenance of divorced wives in the Shah Bano case [1985 (2) SCC 556] was conducted in the context of the Muslim Personal Law (Shariat) Application Act, 1937, whis is applicable to Muslims. The court said that there is nothing in the Muslim Personal Law in which there is some contradiction in the provisions of the maintenance of women, but in this matter, the Central Government completely surrendered and by amending the constitution, surrendered to the clerics.

This constitution is completely based on Hindu culture and Hindu traditions, whose aim has been to allow people to lead a regular life and to provide equal opportunities to all. Reservation was introduced in the constitution to end the evil of Untouchability and high and low in Hinduism because its author Babasaheb Dr. Ambedkar believed that reservation was not just a facility, but a socio-political necessity. When our constitution was prepared, Babasaheb was so impressed by the three words – liberty, equality, and fraternity that he included them in the Preamble of the Constitution of India. Although these words were taken from the French Revolution, they have also been at the core of ancient Hindu philosophy and our constitutional structure stands on the basis of these three words.

Babasaheb Bhimrao Ambedkar did not use the words 'socialist' or 'secular' in the Preamble of the constitution, probably because these words are inherently self-contained in Hindu culture and there is no need to include them separately. But unfortunately, in 1975, the Congress government added these words through 42nd Amendment of the constitution with the aim of Muslim appeasement. The first word of the Preamble is 'sovereign', which means capable of maintaining independence. We can proudly say that India is the only country in the world which exists in its original form despite facing all kinds of invasions on its territory since time immemorial. Thinking of these things, Dr. Ambedkar particularly used this word because he believed that the culture of India is the oldest sovereign civilisation.

The second word he used in the Preamble is 'democracy'. Everyone will accept the fact that democracy is embedded in the basic nature of Indian society. If we look at the ancient history of India, then it can be said that who can be more democratic than Maryada Purushottam Rama? When the person sitting at the last rung of the society's ladder (a washerman) raised his finger on Sita Mata, Rama forced his life-loving wife to undergo an ordeal. Keeping in mind the ancient cultural values of India, Babasaheb Ambedkar prepared the Preamble of the constitution. The third word in the Preamble is 'republic'. He used it because he knew that there is an Anubhav Mandap established by Saint Basavanna in the 12th century and it is the world's oldest republic in India.

The Constitution of India is both workable and sacred in nature. Babasaheb believed that the Constitution of India is not a written document but is an effective tool through which justice can be given to all sections of the society. The effective manner in which Babasaheb performed his role to achieve the rights provided in the Indian Constitution, especially for the oppressed, deprived and downtrodden section of the society, is something to be admired. Articles 14, 15 and 17 of the Constitution of India grant equal rights to every Indian and protect them from discrimination. Under article 17, Untouchability is completely abolished and provides dignity to every citizen. With the aim of giving a defined and decent life to every Indian citizen, Babasaheb included the basic fundamental rights. He mentioned the importance of fundamental rights in his opening remarks too. While the Constituent Assembly has given the right to equality through Articles 14, 15, 16, 17 and 18, similarly right to freedom has been granted to individuals under Articles 19, 20, 21 and 22, whereas the right against exploitation is given under Articles 23 and 24. Under Articles 25, 26, 27 and 28, the right to religious freedom is provided to people residing within the territories of India.

Babasaheb believed that social unity is necessary for any democracy to flourish. From this point of view, Articles 29 and 30 entitle Indian citizens, especially minorities, to voluntarily set up institutions under social and educational rights. He used to say that education is not just a means of earning a living; it is necessary for the overall development of an individual. That is why he emphasised that everyone should be given compulsory education. To grant equality to men and women, Dr. Ambedkar introduced social security by giving the right to adoption and the right to property. Social security to women was part of Ambedkar's vision and to ensure this, Prime Minister Narendra Modi started the 'Beti Bachao, Beti Padhao' campaign in a move to show his commitment to the constitution. Dr. Ambedkar wanted equality for all and talked about taking everyone along.

The family background in which Babasaheb was born was a family of a purely religious nature and during his childhood, he regularly read the *Ramayana* and the *Mahabharata*. That is why the constitution he created was completely based on Hindu culture and traditions. That is why, at the last moment, when he, enraged by the evils of Hinduism, made up his mind to renounce Hinduism, he converted to Buddhism. He even rejected a blank cheque offered to him by the Nizam of Hyderabad to embrace Islam, because he did not want to separate from the mainstream of Hindutva. Embracing Buddhism was only his symbolic show of resistance.

□

Dr. Ambedkar was Strong Supporter of Sanskrit

On 11th September, 1949, a news titled 'Ambedkar with Sanskrit' was published in the *National Herald* newspaper. According to the news, India's Law Minister Dr. Ambedkar was among those who were advocating introduction of Sanskrit as the official language of the Indian Union. Babasaheb believed that Sanskrit was the only language that could ensue linguistic unity of the country. He suggested making it the official language in the country. In the Constituent Assembly, he supported Sanskrit as the national language though he believed that after the country's Independence, English should be retained as the official language of the country for at least 15 years, until Sanskrit became a fully accepted language. Ambedkar had suggested to the Official Languages Commission constituted soon after Independence to make Sanskrit the official language of the Indian Union. He was apprehensive that Independent India might get lost in a linguistic conflict and did not want any dispute regarding language in the country. Now the time has come to select Sanskrit as the official language as it would be respected by all the language-speaking people. Babasaheb knew there was a strong possibility of Sanskrit being considered as the mother of all Indian languages. He was confident that there would be no dispute anywhere in the country regarding the choice of Sanskrit. That is why, when the debate on making any one of the Indian languages as the official language was held, Ambedkar proposed Sanskrit as the official language.

In this proposal, the Deputy Minister of the Ministry of External Affairs of India, B.V. Keskar and a Member of Parliament from Bengal, named Naziruddin Ahmed, were included. Dr. Ambedkar said that the Legislative Council should also consider this while considering the official language. Apart from Babasaheb Ambedkar, Pt. Lakshmikant Maitre (Bengal) and T.T. Krishnamachari (Madras), there were 15 other people whose names were suggested. They were G.S. Guha (Tripura), V. Ramaiah (Pudukkottai), V.I. Munnisama Pillai (Madras), Kallur Subbarao (Madras), V.C. Kesavarao (Madras), D. Govindadasa (Madras), P. Subbarao (Madras), P. Subramaniam (Madras), Durgabai (Madras) and Dashrayani Velayudhana (Madras).

There were three-pointers in the proposal that Dr. Ambedkar submitted to the government of Pandit Jawaharlal Nehru. The first was to make Sanskrit the language of the Union of India; second was to allow English to be continued to be used as the official language for the first 15 years of Independence, while Sanskrit should also be used as a parallel official language. After 15 years, Sanskrit should be made the official language of the Union. The third point of the proposal was that Parliament should make a law to use English only for 15 years. These suggestions of Dr. Ambedkar called for the amendment of the proposal in which the Official Languages Commission had already given its three proposals to the government in August 1949. The council had decided in its resolution that Hindi should be replaced by English and that it would not take more than 10 years to become the official language. The provinces of the Indian Union were made free to use their own regional languages. But the teaching of two languages was necessary in the teaching method of these provinces. It is also the decision of the Council that the Indian Union should use Sanskrit in mottos, titles, etc. and in places of decoration.

It is also a historical truth that Dr. Ambedkar had studied deeply all the texts, *Vedas*, *Puranas*, etc., which had been written in Sanskrit. On the basis of his study, an ideas formed in his mind about Indian culture and he concluded that the Aryans and Dravidians were the original descendants of India and they did not come from outside. Babasaheb wanted to break the misconception that the Aryans had come from outside and to learn which the people of India had to compulsorily read Sanskrit. If the people were to understand Sanskrit, then many discrepancies would be removed. But, unfortunately, this dream of Babasaheb remains incomplete even today.

Babasaheb had respect for the Sanskrit language in his heart. He wanted Sanskrit to become the mother tongue of the nation, but his suggested amendment for introduction of Sanskrit language was not accepted. He wanted the Sanskrit language to become the language of the common people rather than the language of a particular section of the country. But in the Eighth Schedule of the Constitution, it was given a place as a language only. Dr. Ambedkar's dedication to Sanskrit can be understood in this context that, when the national language was being discussed in the Central Hall, people were pleasantly surprised to notice Dr. Ambedkar and Laxmikant Maitre conversing in impeccable Sanskrit among themselves.

It is generally propagated that Dr. Ambedkar was anti-Brahmin but it was not so. In fact, he was opposed to Brahmanism and not to Brahmins. Famous social worker and Rashtriya Swayamsevak Sangh Pracharak Dattopant Thengdi's book titled, *Dr. Ambedkar aur Samajik Kranti ki Yatra* mentions such incidents from which it becomes clear that many Brahmins had a hand in the success of Dr. Ambedkar. Dr. Ambedkar has written, in his autobiography, that a Brahmin teacher named Ambedkar used to teach in his school and make Babasaheb sit with him and also feed him. That teacher gave Babasaheb the nickname 'Ambedkar'. A strange incident occurred with Babasaheb while acting as a guide to the Hindu Code Bill. There was no one to support him at that time. Then two Brahmin Members of Parliament, Hridaynath Kunzru and N.V. Gadgil, gave a speech in the Lok Sabha in his support. In fact, Dr. Ambedkar was ideal not only for one caste or one society, but for the entire humanity and Indianness.

□

Ambedkar and Syama Prasad Mookerjee's Views on One Nation, One Law

(Ek Vidhan-Ek Pradhan-Ek Nishan)

When the country became Independent and Jawaharlal Nehru became the first Prime Minister of the country, three non-Congress members also took oath as cabinet ministers in his cabinet. These ministers included Dr. Bhimrao Ambedkar, who was made the Law Minister as he was a lawyer and legal expert. He was also appointed chairman of the Drafting Committee; Dr. Syama Prasad Mookerjee, a famous politician from Bengal, was leader of the Hindu Mahasabha; and the third minister was R.K. Shanmukham Chetty, who was a Madras merchant and expert in economic matters. Out of these ministers, Dr. Syama Prasad Mookerjee was in opposition to two legislations, two heads and two symbols in one country, which ultimately happened due to the imposition of Article 370, on Nehru's insistence, in Jammu & Kashmir, despite Dr. Ambedkar's aversion. Dr. Mookerjee went to hoist the tricolour in Kashmir and died there under mysterious cicrumstances. Thus with the slogan of 'Ek Nishan, Ek Pradhan, Ek Vidhan', Dr. Mookerjee became the first martyr to liberate Kashmir from the Kashmir movement. The reality is also that if Dr. Mookerjee had not belonged to Bengal, then in the partition of 1947, the whole of Bengal would have become East Pakistan. Angered by the ruthless killing of millions of Hindus in Pakistan and Nehru's anti-India policy on Jammu & Kashmir, Dr. Syama Prasad Mookerjee resigned from the Nehru cabinet and decided to form a nationalist party.

Dr. Syama Prasad Mookerjee and the then Sarsanghchalak of the Rashtriya Swayamsevak Sangh (RSS), Guru Golwalkar, met at the Sangh office in Calcutta and it was decided that the Sangh would give its few workers to help Dr. Mookerjee in his work. Among the workers who were sent from the Sangh to the Jana Sangh were Pt. Deendayal Upadhyay, Atal Bihari Vajpayee, Nanaji Deshmukh, Bhai Mahavir, Sundar Singh Bhandari, Jagannath Rao Joshi, Kushabhau Thackeray were prominent and thus for the unity and prosperity of the nation, Jana Sangh was established while fighting for the unity and integrity of the nation, Dr. Syama Prasad Mookerjee was martyred in Kashmir on 23rd June, 1953, under mysterious circumstances. Unfortunately, the case was not investigated by the government and since then, the issue of the integrity of the country was linked to the Jana Sangh and later to the Bharatiya Janata Party.

Babasaheb Dr. Ambedkar, the second non-Congress member of the Nehru cabinet, proved his mettle as a constitution maker. The most important thing which was the core of his concept of social equality was the Uniform Civil Code, the making of which started even before Independence. He also played an important role in getting it passed. Meanwhile, after differences of opinion with Nehru on this issue, non-cooperation and opposition from Muslims, he abandoned this idea and made tireless efforts to make the Uniform Code (Hindu Code) for Hindus. What a tragedy that the Uniform Code of Conduct which should have been made 70 years ago has not been made even today and the Supreme Court had to comment on it. It is good that at least now the government is considering the introduction of Uniform Civil Code.

Dr. Ambedkar initially received support for the Hindu Code Bill, but later, rather than Hindu Code Bill, the Hindu Marriage and Guardianship Act, 1956, was enacted for the Hindus, and the legal inequalities prevailing among the Hindus were considered to be legally cognisable offences.

This was the last effort of Babasaheb while in power to bring down the important topic of one nation, one law, and Article 44 of his constitution and the basic spirit of social equality and justice. He resigned from the Nehru cabinet in October 1951, even before the Hindu Code Bill.

It can be clearly seen that after the partition of the country on religious lines, in 1947, white pigeons of incomplete independence continued to be flown in Jammu & Kashmir till the sixties, but which were coloured by the blood of Dr. Syama Prasad Mookerjee. After giving constitutional ground to one nation, one law in the country, Babasaheb Ambedkar showed the path through a 'Uniform Civil Code and Hindu Code' in the fifties. The BJP-led NDA government at the Centre has abolished Article 370 and sought the opinion from the National Law Commission, which is the country's highest legislative advisory body on the Uniform Civil Code.

Since Independence, the Supreme Court of India has been showing its commitment from time to time on these subjects and the result has been that the controversial provisions of Triple Talaq, Article 370 and Article 35A are now abolished, and everyone in the country is looking forward to the Uniform Civil Code. The Supreme Court of India has sought the views of the Government of India on its commitment to the Uniform Civil Code.

Architect of Constitution Babasaheb Dr. Ambedkar

and Dr. Syama Prasad Mookerjee, of course, had different ideologies on economic and social issues, but both were of the same ideology in the matter of national unity and integrity. While Dr. Mookerjee sacrificed his life in protest against Article 370, Babasaheb Ambedkar resigned from the Nehru cabinet for not accepting his word on Article 370 and the Uniform Code of Conduct. Babasaheb Ambedkar, the architect of the constitution, was a staunch nationalist besides being an expert of law.

Famous historian Durgadas in his book, *India from Curzon to Nehru and After* writes on p, 236 that, 'He was nationalist to the core.' His biggest concern was to give respect to the Dalits and the Untouchables of India by empowering them. He never compromised on this subject but not at the cost of dividing the Hindu society.

As a matter of fact, the real issue on which Dr. Ambedkar was most upset with the Hindu Code Bill was that the Nehru government did not discuss it till 1951, by which time, Babasaheb's patience had run out and he resigned from the Nehru cabinet. Had the Hindu Code Bill been made under Ambedkar's guidance, it would have had a different form, leaving no aspect of social justice. In 1954, in the absence of Dr. Ambedkar, Nehru's Hindu Code Bill came, in which a nationwide law could not be made. Both Dr. Ambedkar and Dr. Syama Prasad Mookerjee were actually in favour of the Uniform Civil Code and opposed Article 370. If the Nehru government had accepted both of these, then India would have been a country of modern, scientific thinking and rational thoughts. Unfortunately, both these great leaders had to resign from Nehru's cabinet upon seeing these crucial issues of national importance being ignored. However, Prime Minister Narendra Modi is determined to make the dreams of these two great leaders come true.

Very few people know that upon these issues, Babasaheb and Balraj Madhok, who was the president of Jana Sangh in the year 1966 and the nurturer of Hindutva, got close and Balraj Madhok would often meet Dr. Ambedkar at 26 Alipur Road.

□

Struggle for Putting Ambedkar's Portrait in Principal's Office

When a new Lok Sabha is formed after the Lok Sabha elections, according to the constitutional structure, the members have to take an oath and the newly elected MPs take oath in the name of their respective deities. In the 17th Lok Sabha, it was special that the members raised slogans of their respective great personalities and *ishta devatas*, and perhaps this was seen for the first time in the parliamentary history of India. When the name of Asaduddin Owaisi, who is always in the discussions amidst his eloquent speeches, was called for oath-taking in the House, at that time, slogans of 'Bharat Mata ki Jai' started resonating in the house. He took the oath in Urdu and then raised slogans of 'Jai Bhim', 'Jai Bhim', 'Jai Bhim', 'Allah Hu Akbar' and 'Jai Hind'. Shyam Singh Yadav, who won from the Bahujan Party, raised slogans of 'Jai Bhim', 'Jai Bharat' and 'Jai Ambedkar'. During the elections, a TV journalist asked Owaisi, 'The BJP has nationalism, what do you have? In response, he said, 'I have the constitution given by Babasaheb' and his reply surprised the people. The person who would have first raised the slogan of 'Jai Bhim' would have never imagined that the slogan of 'Jai Bhim' would ever resonate in the corridors of Parliament. While the goal of the oath-taking MPs was to make the nation paramount, at the same time, they had to salute

Babasaheb Ambedkar, the architect of the constitution, for his incomparable contributions.

Before taking oath this time, Prime Minister Narendra Modi organised a special event to honour the historic Constitution of India. For all of us, the dignity of the Indian Constitution and the unity of the nation are supreme. Earlier in the 16th Lok Sabha, a special session was held in the Lok Sabha on the occasion of the 125th birth anniversary of Babasaheb. Today, everyone says that if Babasaheb's thoughts had been imbibed with sincerity, then the problems of the country would have been solved automatically. The growing gap between the rich and the poor would have ended long ago and everyone would have received employment, housing, education, health and self-respect. It is meant to say that today the whole environment has become Ambedkarite.

It was 1971 when the India-Pakistan war was going on and I was a student of Class IX. There was a debate going on between some Brahmin teachers and Yadav teachers regarding the war. Some Yadav teachers took a jibe at the then Defence Minister Babu Jagjivan Ram and said that for how many days will 'Chamar' Defence Minister fight? It is the charisma of Babasaheb Dr. Ambedkar that after six decades of his death, Dalit-Muslim-OBC unity is talked about in the fight for social justice. In those days, the name of Dr. Ambedkar as the architect of the constitution was discussed very secretly among the Dalits. No one had the courage to say in front of the entire society that the constitution was composed by Babasaheb Dr. Ambedkar, who was chairman of the Drafting Committee of the constitution. Hence he contributed the most among the members and the following data shows which member spoke how many words:

Sr. No.	Name	No. of Words Spoken
1.	B.R. Ambedkar	2,67,544
2.	T.T. Krishnamachari	97,638
3.	A. Krishnaswami Ayyar	61,612
4.	K.M. Munshi	60,056
5.	Gopalaswami Ayyangar	56,025
6.	Muhammad Sadulla	19,868
7.	Devi Pramod Khaitan	4927
8.	N. Madhav Rao	3046
9.	V.L. Mittar	2811

But due to the social status at that time, his contribution was not openly accepted by the people. Yes, there was one more thing that people of a petty mentality who opposed reservation used to talk about was about burning the constitution composed by Ambedkar. A positive thing was happening at that time – the youth and students were openly celebrating Ambedkar's birthday and Parinirvana Day. This was part of the social consciousness and the Dalits of the village had stopped picking up dead animals. Because Babasaheb Ambedkar had converted to Buddhism sometime before his death, marriages of Dalit youths and young women started taking place in the Buddhist manner and without involving the ritualistic Brahmins.

Emergency was imposed in the country in 1975 and all Opposition leaders were imprisoned. At this time, Prime Minister Indira Gandhi launched a 20-point programme to increase her popularity and liberated the landless farmers and Dalits from the clutches of moneylenders. Banks had been nationalised only a few years before this. We can criticise the

Emergency in many aspects, but the era of Emergency should be appreciated for giving freedom to bonded labours, freedom from the exploitation of moneylenders and an unusual rise in Dalit consciousness and awakening. There has been a lot of progress. The Emergency ended, the Janata Party government was formed and the Students' Union was restored in the colleges. I got elected in the Students' Union team of my college. Some of my friends suggested that the picture of Babasaheb Ambedkar should also be placed in the principal's office along with the picture of Gandhiji and other leaders. At that time I was a student at Mariyahu Degree College, in Jaunpur district. Being a student leader, I went to Shri Gauri Shankar Mishra, the principal of the college, with the proposal of putting a portrait of Dr. Ambedkar in his office. The principal was a very learned person and a thorough gentleman. He approved the proposal for Dr. Ambedkar's portrait, but from the look on his face, it seemed that he was not happy with this proposal. After much hesitation and a lot of pressure, finally, Dr. Ambedkar's portrait was placed there. When I passed out from the college in 1978, I got to know that Babasaheb's portrait had been removed from the principal's office.

It is true that today, every political party and every leader does not hesitate to say 'Jai Bhim'. Today Ambedkar and 'Jai Bhim' have become the symbols of our society and politics and in 1989-90, the government of the late Vishwanath Pratap Singh honoured him with the Bharat Ratna. On his 125th birth anniversary, a special session was organised in the Parliament. All the memories related to him, such as 26 Alipore Road, Delhi, his birthplace in Mhow and the London house where he lived and studied, have been given a grand appearance. The Ambedkar International Centre has been established in New Delhi. Prime Minister Narendra Modi seems determined to realise the India of his dreams, his 'Jan Dhan Yojana' and

'Ujjwala Yojana' are playing an important role in bringing women and the underprivileged into the mainstream of the nation, but the struggle, that was fought for a long time to take Babasaheb's principles and ideas to the masses, is unforgettable.

To carry forward his basic *mantra* of being educated and staying united, many Dalits and deprived society leaders have sacrificed their lives, about which we do not know at all. However, the real tribute to such hardworking social workers would be to build a healthy society by following the constitution made by Babasaheb and the path shown by him.

□

Dalit-Muslim Alliance of Jogendra Nath Mandal and Jinna was a Betrayal

If you give attention on the facts of formation of Pakistan, it will come to your mind that the formation of Pakistan would have not been possible if an alliance would not have happened between famous dalit leader Jogendra Nath Mandal and Mohd. Ali Jinna. During freedom struggle, Mohd. Ali Jinna established himself as a communal Muslim leader whereas Jogendra Nath Mandal rose as a dalit leader as a contemporary and as effective to Dr. B.R. Ambedkar. He wanted to have 40% Hindu population which consisted of 90% dalits to remain in East Pakistan where as Baba Saheb wanted a complete transfer of population after partition. In fact Shri J.N. Mandal was political guide of Dr. Ambedkar and he was instrumental in sending Dr. Ambedkar in parliament by asking him to contest from Bengal. Though Dr. Ambedkar was always saying that Dalit-Muslim alliance is nothing but a step to betray dalits. In his book "Thoughts on Pakistan, he wrote that Muslims are against social reforms. Muslim can never be brotherly and affectionate for non-Muslims. He further wrote-In such situation, we should allow formation of Pakistan but before the partition, we should plan complete transfer of population on religion basis. Because it is not possible for non-Muslims to live peacefully, honourably without any discrimination in Muslim majority areas. It is a well known fact that the first experiment of Dalit-Muslim alliance was done by Mr. Mandal with Jinna. Jinna was successful in formation of Pakistan by giving false assurance of safety to those Hindus who will remain in Pakistan but later on he refrained from even picking the phone calls of Jogendra Nath Mandal.

Jinna used dalits in formation of Pakistan and encouraged them to remain in Pakistan because he wanted to use them as a tool to fulfil the requirements of rich Muslims. All his claims for welfare of these minority Hindus proved to be false and mischieveous. In undivided India, 40% Hindu population of East Bengal (Now Bangladesh) vote in favour of Pakistan and Pakistan came in to existence because of Dalit-Muslim alliance but soon after formation of Pakistan, this alliance was finished. After formation of Pakistan, Mandal's dream of a good and dignified honourable life for dalits was shattered because Jinna used him with ulterior motive. Though on 15th August, 1947 after partition of India, Mandal became the temporary President of the Constitution Committee and thereafter became the Law and Labour Minister of Pakistan and continued to look after the Ministry upto 1950. Later he realised that Jinna was neither successful in stopping atrocies on dalits in Pakistan nor did he even try to stop such heinous act Mandal could not forget the atrocities on poor dalits and very shortly he realised the reality of Dalit-Muslim alliance. He was able to understand the betrayal with him and the dalit society by Jinna and his associates. Ultimately under distress and depression, he resigned on 8th October, 1950 from the cabinet and returned to India. He remained in Bangoan, West Bengal and never returned to Pakistan and after exile of 18 years, he died on 5th October, 1968. During his last days, he understood that he did a blunder by relying on Dalit-Muslim alliance. The rich and high caste Hindus came to West Bengal but 32% still remained there in which 90% were dalits but the 32% Hindus population in 1950 was reduced to only 8.5%. Dalits were not allowed to leave Pakistan and forced to live as slaves and most of the Hindus were forced to convert to Mulims. Ultimately Mandal reached to a conclusion that his belief in Dalit-Muslim alliance resulted into worse condition of crores of Hindus in Pakistan and his thoughts about the atrocities on non-Muslims in Pakistan were reflected in his 20 page resignation written to Prime Minister of Pakistan which is appended here. If our Hindu organisations had if our Hindu organisations had publicised vasty his poignant and excessively painful his experience to India, we could have avoided many experiences among Indians, incidents against the country such as JNU campus, Shahin Bagh etc. where illusioned youths with support of Congress and left parties shouted slogans like 'Bharat tere tukde honge Insha Allah, Insha-Allah'.

Resignation of Jogendra Nath Mandal as Law Minister of Pakistan

My dear Prime Minister

It is with a heavy heart and a sense of utter frustration at the failure of my lifelong mission to uplift the backward Hindu masses of East Bengal that I feel compelled to tender resignation of my membership of your cabinet. It is proper that I should set forth in detail the reasons which have prompted me to take this decision at this important juncture of the Indo-Pakistani subcontinent. It is to share just a truth

1. Before I narrate the remote and immediate causes of my resignation, it may be useful to give a short background of the important events that have taken place during the period of

my co-operation with the League. Having been approached by a few prominent League leaders of Bengal in February 1943, I agreed to work with them in the Bengal Legislative Assembly. After the fall of the Fazlul Haq ministry in March 1943, with a party of 21 Scheduled Caste M.L.A.s, I agreed to cooperate with Khwaja Nazimuddin, the then leader of the Muslim League Parliamentary Party who formed the Cabinet in April 1943. Our co-operation was conditional on certain specific terms, such as the inclusion of three Scheduled Caste Ministers in the Cabinet, sanctioning of a sum of Rupees Five Lakhs as annual recurring grant for the education of the Scheduled Castes, and the unqualified application of the communal ratio rules in the matter of appointment to Government services.

2. Apart from these terms, the principal objectives that prompted me to work in co-operation with the Muslim League was, first that the economic interests of the Muslims in Bengal were generally identical with those of the Scheduled Castes. Muslims were mostly cultivators and labourers, and so were members of the Scheduled Castes. One section of Muslims were fishermen, so was a section of the Scheduled Castes as well, and secondly that the Scheduled Castes and the Muslims were both educationally backward. I was persuaded that my co-operation with the League and its Ministry would lead to the undertaking on a wide scale of legislative and administrative measures which, while promoting the mutual welfare of the vas bulk of Bengal's population, and undermining the foundations of vested interest and privilege, would further the cause of communal peace and harmony. It may be mentioned here that Khwaja Nazimuddin took three Scheduled Caste Ministers in his cabinet and appointed three Parliamentary Secretaries from amongst the members of my community.

Suhrawardy Ministry

3. After the general elections held in March 1946 Mr. H.S. Suhrawardy became the leader of the League Parliamentary Party in March 1946 and formed the League Ministry in April 1946. I was the only Scheduled Caste member returned on the federation ticket. I was included in Mr. Suhrawardy's Cabinet. The 16th day of August of that year was observed in Calcutta as 'The Direct Action Day' by the Muslim League. It resulted, as you know, in a holocaust. Hindus demanded my resignation from the League Ministry. My life was in peril. I began to receive threatening letters almost every day. But I remained steadfast to my policy. Moreover, I issued an appeal through our journal 'Jagaran' to the Scheduled Caste people to keep themselves aloof from the bloody feud between the Congress and the Muslim League even at the risk of my life. I cannot but gratefully acknowledge the fact that I was saved from the wrath of infuriated Hindu mobs by my Caste Hindu neighbours. The Calcutta carnage was followed by the 'Noakhali Riot' in October 1946. There, Hindus including Scheduled Castes were killed and hundreds were converted to Islam. Hindu women were raped and abducted. Members of my community also suffered loss of life and property. Immediately after these happenings, I visited Tipperah and Feni and saw some riot-affected areas. The terrible sufferings of Hindus overwhelmed me with grief, but still I continued the policy of co-operation with the Muslim League. Immediately after the massive Calcutta Killing, a no-confidence motion was moved against the Suhrawardy Ministry. It was only due to my efforts that the support of four Anglo-Indian Members and of four Scheduled Caste members of the Assembly who had hitherto been with the Congress could be secured, but for which the Ministry would have been defeated.

4. In October 1946, most unexpectedly came to me

through Mr. Suhrawardy the offer of a seat in the Interim Government of India. After a good deal of hesitation and being given only one hour's time to take my final decision, I consented to accept the offer subject to the condition only that I should be permitted to resign if my leader Dr. B.R. Ambedkar disapproved of my action. Fortunately, however, I received his approval in a telegram sent from London. Before I left for Delhi to take over as Law Member, I persuaded Mr. Suhrawardy, the then Chief Minister of Bengal, to agree to take two Ministers in his Cabinet in my place and to appoint two Parliamentary Secretaries from the Scheduled Case Federation Group.

5. I joined the Interim Government on 1st November, 1946. After about a month when I paid a visit to Calcutta, Mr. Suhrawardy apprised me of the communal tension in some parts of East Bengal, especially in Gopalganj Sub-division, where the Namahsudras were in majority, being very high. He requested me to visit those areas and address meetings of Muslims and Namahsudras. The fact was that Namahsudras in those areas had made preparations for retaliation. I addressed about a dozen of largely attended meetings. The result was that Namahsudras gave up the idea of retaliation. Thus an inevitable dangerous communal disturbance was averted.

6. After a few months, the British Government made their June 3 Statement (1947) embodying certain proposals for the partition of India. The whole country, especially the entire non-Muslim India, was startled. For the sake of truth I must admit that I had always considered the demand of Pakistan by the Muslim League as a bargaining counter. Although I honestly felt that in the context of India as a whole Muslims had legitimate cause for grievance against upper class Hindu chauvinism, I held the view very strongly indeed that the creation of Pakistan would never solve the communal problem. On the contrary, it would aggravate communal hatred and

bitterness. Besides, I maintained that it would not ameliorate the condition of Muslims in Pakistan. The inevitable result of the partition of the country would be to prolong, if not perpetuate, the poverty, illiteracy and miserable condition of the toiling masses of both the States. I further apprehended that Pakistan might turn to be one of the most backward and undeveloped countries of the South East Asia.

Lahore Resolution

7. I must make it clear that I have thought that an attempt would be made, as is being done at present, to develop Pakistan as a purely 'Islamic' State based on the Shariat and the injunctions and formulae of Islam. I presumed that it would be set up in all essentials after the pattern contemplated in the Muslim League resolution adopted at Lahore on March 23, 1940. That resolution stated inter alia that (I) "geographically contiguous areas are demarcated into regions which should be constituted with such territorial readjustments as may be necessary, that the areas in which the Muslims are numerically in majority as in the north-western and eastern zones of India, should be grouped to constitute independent States in which the Constituent units shall be autonomous and sovereign" and (II) "adequate, effective and mandatory safeguards should be specifically provided in the Constitution for minorities in these units and in these regions for the protection of their religious, cultural, political, administrative and other rights and interests in consultation with them." Implicitly in this formula were (a) that North western and eastern Muslim zones should be constituted into two independent States, (b) that the constituent units of these States should be autonomous and sovereign, (c) that minorities' guarantee should be in respect of rights as well as of interest and extend to every sphere of their lives, and (d) that Constitutional provisions should be

made in these regards in consultation with the minorities themselves. I was fortified in my faith in this resolution and the professions of the League Leadership by the statement Qaid-e-Azam Mohammed Ali Jinnah was pleased to make on the 11th August 1947 as the President of the Constituent Assembly giving solemn assurance of equal treatment for Hindus & Muslims alike and calling upon them to remember that they were all Pakistanis. There was then no question of dividing he people on the basis of religion into full-fledged Muslim citizens and zimmies [i][1] being under the perpetual custody of the Islamic State and its Muslims citizens. Every one of these pledges is being flagrantly violated apparently to your knowledge and with your approval in complete disregard of the Qaid-e-Azam's wishes and sentiments and to the detriment and humiliation of the minorities.

Partition Of Bengal

8. It may also be mentioned in this connection that I was opposed to the partition of Bengal. In launching a campaign in this regard I had to face not only tremendous resistance from all quarters but also unspeakable abuse, insult and dishonour. With great regret, I recollect those days when 32 crores of Hindus of this Indo-Pakistan Sub-continent turned their back against me and dubbed me as the enemy of Hindus and Hinduism, but I remained undaunted and unmoved in my loyalty to Pakistan. It is a matter of gratitude that my appeal to 7 million Scheduled Caste people of Pakistan evoked a ready and enthusiastic response from them. They lent me their unstinted support sympathy and encouragement.

9. After the establishment of Pakistan on 14th August, 1947 you formed the Pakistan Cabinet, in which I was included and Khwaja Nazimuddin formed a provisional Cabinet for East Bengal. On August 10, I had spoken to Khwaja Nazimuddin at

Karachi and requested him to take 2 Scheduled Caste Ministers in the East Bengal Cabinet. He promised to do the same sometime later. What happened subsequently in this regard was a record of unpleasant and disappointing negotiation with you, Khwaja Nazimuddin and Mr. Nurul Amin, the present Chief Minister of East Bengal. When I realised that Khwaja Nazimuddin was avoiding the issue on this or that excuse, I became almost impatient and exasperated. I further discussed the matter with the Presidents of the Pakistan Muslim League and its East Bengal Branch. Ultimately, I brought the matter to your notice. You were pleased to discuss the subject with Khwaja Nazimuddin in my presence at your residence. Khwaja Nazimuddin agreed to take one Scheduled Caste Minister on his return to Dacca. As I had already becamesceptic about the assurance of Khwaja Nazimuddin, I wanted to be definite about the time-frame. I insisted that he must act in this regard with a month, failing which I should be at liberty to resign. Both you and Khwaja Nazimuddin agreed to the condition. But alas! you did not perhaps mean what you said. Khwaja Nazimuddin did not keep his promise. After Mr. Nurul Amin had became the Chief Minister of East Bengal, I again took up the matter with him. He also followed the same old familiar tactics of evasion. When I again called your attention to this matter prior to your visit to Dacca in 1949, you were pleased to assure me that Minority Ministers would be appointed in East Bengal, and you asked 2/3 names from me for consideration. In stat deference to your wish, I sent you a note stating the Federation Group in the East Bengal Assembly and suggesting three names. When I made enquiries as to what had happened on your return from Dacca, you appeared to be very cold and only remarked : "Let Nurul Amin return from Delhi". After a few days I again pressed the matter. But you avoided the issue. I was then forced to come to the conclusion that neither you not Mr. Nurul Amin had any intention to take any Scheduled Caste Minister in the East Bengal Cabinet. Apart from this, I was noticing that Mr. Nurul Amin and some League leaders of East Bengal were trying to create disruption among the Members of the Scheduled Caste Federation. It appeared to me that my leadership and wide-spread popularity were considered ominous. My outspokenness, vigilance and sincere efforts to safeguard the interests of the minorities of Pakistan, in general, and of the Scheduled Caste, in particular, were considered a matter on annoyance to the East Bengal Govt. and few League leaders. Undaunted, I took my firm stand to safeguard the interests of the minorities of Pakistan.

Anti-Hindu Policy

10. When the question of partition of Bengal arose, the Scheduled Caste people were alarmed at the anticipated dangerous result of partition. Representation on their behalf were made to Mr. Suhrawardy, the then Chief Minister of Bengal who was pleased to issue a statement to the press declaring that none of the rights and privileges hitherto enjoyed by the Scheduled Caste People would be curtailed after partition and that they would not only continue to enjoy the existing rights and privileges but also receive additional advantages. This assurance was given by Mr. Suhrawardy not only in his personal capacity but also in his capacity as the Chief Minister of the League Ministry. To my utter regret it is to be stated that after partition, particularly after the death of Qaid-e-Azam, the Scheduled Castes have not received a fair deal in any matter. You will recollect that from time to time I brought the grievances of the Scheduled Castes to your notice. I explained to you on several occasions the nature of inefficient administration in East Bengal. I made serious charges against the police administration. I brought to your notice incidents

of barbarous atrocities perpetrated by the police on frivolous grounds. I did not hesitate to bring to your notice the anti-Hindu policy pursued by the East Bengal Government especially the police administration and a section of Muslim League leaders.

Some Incidents

11. The first incident that shocked me took place at a village called Digharkul near Gopalganj where on the false complaint of a Muslim brutal atrocities were committed on the local Namahsudras. The fact was that a Muslim who was going in a boat attempted to throw his net to catch fish. A Namahsudra who was already there for the same purpose opposed the throwing of the net in his front. This was followed by some altercation and the Muslim got annoyed and went to the nearby Muslim village and made a false complaint that he and a woman in his boat had been assaulted by the Namahsudras. At that time, the S.D.O. of Gopalganj was passing in a boat through the canal, who without making any enquiry accepted the complaint as true and sent armed police to the spot to punish the Namahsudras. The armed police came and the local Muslims also joined them. They not only raided some houses of the Namahsudras but mercilessly beat both men and women, destroyed their properties and took away valuables. The merciless beating of a pregnant women resulted in abortion on the spot. This brutal action on the part of the local authority created panic over a large area.

12. The second incidence of police oppression took place in early part of 1949 under P.S. Gournadi in the district of Barisal. Here a quarrel took place between two groups of members of a Union Board. One group which was in the good books of the police conspired against the opponents on the plea of their being Communists. On the information of a threat of attack on the Police Station, the O.C., Gournadi

requisitioned armed forces from the headquarters. The Police, helped by the armed forces, then raided a large number of houses in the area, took away valuable properties, even from the house of absentee-owners who were never in politics, far less in the Communist Party. A large number of persons over a wide area were arrested. Teachers and students of many High English Schools were Communist suspects and unnecessarily harassed. This area being very near to my native village, I was informed of the incident. I wrote to the District Magistrate and the S.P. for an enquiry. A section of the local people also prayed for an enquiry by the S.D.O. But no enquiry was held. Even my letters to the District authorities were not acknowledged. I then brought this matter to the notice of the highest Authority in Pakistan, including yourself but to no avail.

Women For Military

13. The atrocities perpetrated by the police and the military on the innocent Hindus, especially the Scheduled Castes of Habibgarh in the District of Sylhet deserve description. Innocent men and women were brutally tortured, some women ravished, their houses raided and properties looted by the police and the local Muslims. Military pickets were posted in the area. The military not only oppressed these people and took away stuff forcibly from Hindu houses, but also forced Hindus to send their women-folk at night to the camp to satisfy the carnal desires of the military. This fact also I brought to your notice. You assured me of a report on the matter, but unfortunately no report was forthcoming.

14. Then occurred the incident at the Nachole in the District of Rajshahi where in the name of suppression of Communists not only the police but also the local Muslims in collaboration with the police oppressed the Hindus and looted their properties. The Santhals then crossed the border

and came over to West Bengal. They narrated the stories of atrocities wantonly committed by the Muslims and the police.

15. An instance of callous and cold-blooded brutality is furnished by the incident that took place on December 20, 1949 in Kalshira under P.S. Mollarhat in the District of Khulna. What happened was that late at night four constables raided the house of one Joydev Brahma in village Kalshira in search of some alleged Communists. At the scent of the police, half a dozen of young men, some of whom might have been Communists, escaped from the house. The police constable entered into the house and assaulted the wife of Joydev Brahma whose cry attracted her husband and a few companions who escaped from the house. They became desperate, re-entered the house, found 4 constables with one gun only. That perhaps might have encouraged the young men who struck a blow on an armed constable who died on the spot. The young men then attacked another constable when the other two ran away and raised alarm which attracted some neighbouring people who came to their rescue. As the incident took place before sunrise when it was dark, the assailants fled with the dead body before the villagers could come. The S.P. of Khulna with a contingent of military and armed police appeared on the scene in the afternoon of the following day. In the meantime, the assailants fled and the intelligent neighbours also fled away. But the bulk of the villagers remained in their houses as they were absolutely innocent and failed to realise the consequence of the happening. Subsequently, the S.P., the military and armed police began to beat mercilessly the innocents of the entire village, encouraged the neighbouring Muslims to take away their properties. A number of persons were killed and men and women were forcibly converted. House-hold deities were broken and places of worship desecrated and destroyed. Several women were raped by the police, military and local

Muslims. Thus a veritable hell was let loose not only in the village of Kalshira which is 1-1/2 miles in length with a large population, but also in a number of neighbouring Namahsudra villages. The village Kalshira was never suspected by the authority to be a place of Communist activities. Another village called Jhalardanga, which was at a distance of 3 miles from Kalshira, was known to be a centre of Communist activities. This village was raided by a large contingent of police on that day for hunt of the alleged Communists, a number of whom fled away and took shelter in the aforesaid house of village Kalshira which was considered to be a safe place for them.

16. I visited Kalshira and one or two neighbouring villages on the 28th February 1950. The S.P., Khulna and some of the prominent League leaders of the district were with me. When I came to the village Kalshira, I found the place desolate and in ruins. I was told in the presence of S.P. that there were 350 homesteads in this village, of these, only three had been spared and the rest had been demolished. Country boats and heads of cattle belonging to the Namasudras had been all taken away. I reported these facts to the Chief Minister, Chief Secretary and Inspector of General of Police of East Bengal and to you.

17. It may be mentioned in this connection that the news of this incident was published in West Bengal Press and this created some unrest among the Hindus there. A number of sufferers of Kalshira, both men and women, homeless and destitute had also come to Calcutta and narrated the stories of their sufferings which resulted in some communal disturbances in West Bengal in the last part of January.

Causes of The February Disturbance

18. It must be noted that stories of a few incidents of communal disturbance that took place in West Bengal as a sort of repercussion of the incidents at Kalshira were published

in exaggerated form in he East Bengal press. In the second week of February 1950 when the Budget Session of the East Bengal Assembly commenced, the Congress Members sought permission to move two adjournment motions to discuss the situation created at Kalshira and Nachole. But the motions were disallowed. The Congress members walked out of the Assembly in protest. This action of the Hindu members of the Assembly annoyed and enraged not only the Ministers but also the Muslim leaders and officials of the Province. This was perhaps one of the principal reasons for Dacca and East Bengal riots in February 1950.

19. It is significant that on 10th February, 1950 at about 10 o'clock in the morning a woman was painted with red to show that her breast was cut off in Calcutta riot, and was taken round the East Bengal Secretariat at Dacca. Immediately the Government servants of the Secretariat stuck work and came out in procession raising slogans of revenge against the Hindus. The procession began to swell as it passed over a distance of more than a mile. It ended in a meeting at Victoria Park at about 12 o'clock in the noon where violent speeches against the Hindus were delivered by several speakers, including officials. The fun of the whole show was that while the employees of the Secretariat went out of procession, the Chief Secretary of the East Bengal Government was holding a conference with his West Bengal counterpart in the same building to find out ways and means to stop communal disturbances in the two Bengals.

Officials Helped Looters

20. The riot started at about 1 p.m. simultaneously all over the city. Arson, looting of Hindu shops and houses and killing of Hindus, wherever they were found, commenced in full swing in all parts of the city. I got evidence even from the Muslims that arson and looting were committed even in the

presence of high police officials. Jewellery shops belonging to the Hindus were looted in the presence of police officers. They not only did not attempt to stop loot, but also helped the looters with advice and direction. Unfortunately for me, I reached Dacca at 5 o'clock in the afternoon on the same day, in February10, 1950. To my utter dismay, I had occasion to see and know things from close quarters. What I saw and learnt from firsthand information was simply staggering and heart-rending.

Background of The Riot

21. The reasons for the Dacca riot were mainly five:

(i) To punish the Hindus for the daring action of their representatives in the Assembly in their expression of protest by walking out of the Assembly when two adjournment motions on Kalshira and Nachole affairs were disallowed.

(ii) Dissension and differences between the Suhrawardy Group and the Nazimuddin Group in the Parliamentary Party were becoming acute.

(iii) Apprehension of launching of a movement for re-union of East and West Bengal by both Hindu and Muslim leaders made the East Bengal Ministry and the Muslim League nervous. They wanted to prevent such a move. They though that any large-scale communal riot in East Bengal was sure to produce reactions in West Bengal where Muslims might be killed. The result of such riots in both East and West Bengal, it was believed, would prevent any movement for re-union of Bengals.

(iv) Feeling of antagonism between the Bengali Muslims and non-Bengali Muslims in East Bengal was gaining ground. This could only be prevented by creating hatred between Hindus and Muslims of East Bengal. The language question was also connected with it and

(v) The consequences of non-devaluation and the Indo-Pakistan trade deadlock to the economy of East Bengal were being felt most acutely first in urban and rural areas and the Muslim League members and officials wanted to divert the attention of the Muslim masses from the impending economic breakdown by some sort of Jihad against Hindus.

Staggering Details - Nearly 10,000 Killed

22. During my nine days' stay at Dacca, I visited most of the riot-affected areas of the city and suburbs. I visited Mirpur also under P.S. Tejgaon. The news of the killing of hundreds of innocent Hindus in trains, on railway lines between Dacca and Narayanganj, and Dacca and Chittagong gave me the rudest shock. On the second day of Dacca riot, I met the Chief Minister of East Bengal and requested him to issue immediate instructions to the District authorities to take all precautionary measures to prevent spreading of the riot in district towns and rural areas. On the 20th February 1950, I reached Barisal town and was astounded to know of the happenings in Barisal. In the District town, a number of Hindu houses were burnt and a large number of Hindus killed. I visited almost all riot-affected areas in the District. I was simply puzzled to find the havoc wrought by the Muslim rioters even at places like Kasipur, Madhabpasha and Lakutia which were within a radius of six miles from the District town and were connected with motorable roads. At the Madhabpasha Zamindar's house, about 200 people were killed and 40 injured. A place, called Muladi, witnessed a dreadful hell. At Muladi Bandar alone, the number killed would total more than three hundred, as was

reported to me by the local Muslims including some officers. I visited Muladi village also, where I found skeletons of dead bodies at some places. I found dogs and vultures eating corpses on he river-side. I got the information there that after the whole-scale killing of all adult males, all the young girls were distributed among the ringleaders of the miscreants. At a place called Kaibartakhali under P.S. Rajapur, 63 persons were killed. Hindu houses within a stone's throw distance from the said thana office were looted, burnt and inmates killed. All Hindu shops of Babuganj Bazar were looted and then burnt and a large number of Hindus were killed. From detailed information received, the conservative estimate of casualties was placed at 2,500 killed in the District of Barisal alone. Total casualties of Dacca and East Bengal riot were estimated to be in the neighbourhood of 10,000 killed. The lamentation of women and children who had lost their all including near and dear ones melted my heart. I only asked myself "What was coming to Pakistan in the name of Islam."

No Earnest Desire To Implement Delhi Pact

23. The large scale exodus of Hindus from Bengal commenced in the latter part of March. It appeared that within a short time all the Hindus would migrate to India. A war cry was raised in India. The situation became extremely critical. A national calamity appeared to be inevitable. The apprehended disaster, however, was avoided by the Delhi Agreement of April 8. With a view to reviving the already lost morale of the panicky Hindus, I undertook an extensive tour of East Bengal. I visited a number of places of the districts of Dacca, Barisal, Faridpur, Khulna and Jessore. I addressed dozens of largely attended meetings and asked the Hindus to take courage and not to leave their ancestral hearths and homes. I had this expectation that the East Bengal Govt. and Muslim League

leaders would implement the terms of the Delhi Agreement. But with the lapse of time, I began to realise that neither the East Bengal Govt. nor the Muslim League leaders were really earnest in the matter of implementation of the Delhi Agreement. The East Bengal Govt. was not only ready to set up a machinery as envisaged in the Delhi Agreement, but also was not willing to take effective steps for the purpose. A number of Hindus who returned to native village immediately after the Delhi Agreement were not given possession of their homes and lands which were occupied in the meantime by the Muslims.

Moulana Akram Khan's Incitations

24. My suspicion about the intention of League leaders was confirmed when I read editorial comments by Moulana Akram Khan, the President of the Provincial Muslim League in the "Baisak" issue of a monthly journal called 'Mohammadi'. In commenting on the first radio-broadcast of Dr. A.M. Malik, Minister for Minority Affairs of Pakistan, from Dacca Radio Station, wherein he said, "Even Prophet Mohammed had given religious freedom to the Jews in Arabia", Moulana Akram Khan said, "Dr. Malik would have done well had he not made any reference in his speech to the Jews of Arabia. It is true that the Jews in Arabia had been given religious freedom by Prophet Mohammed; but it was the first chapter of the history. The last chapter contains the definite direction of prophet Mohammed which runs as follows–"Drive away all the Jews out of Arabia". Even despite this editorial comment of a person who held a very high position in the political, social and spiritual life of the Muslim community, I entertained some expectation that the Nurul Amin Ministry might not be so insincere. But that expectation of mine was totally shattered when Mr. Nurul Amin selected D.N. Barari as a Minister to represent the minorities

in terms of the Delhi Agreement which clearly states that to restore confidence in the minds of the minorities one of their representatives will be taken in the Ministry of East Bengal and West Bengal Govt.

Nurul Amin Government's Insincerity

25. In one of my public statement, I expressed the view that the appointment of D.N. Barari as a Minister representing the minorities not only did not help restore any confidence, but, on the contrary, destroyed all expectations illusions, if there was any in the minds of the minorities about the sincerity of Mr. Nurul Amin's Govt. My own reaction was that Mr. Nurul Amin's Govt. was not only insincere but also wanted to defeat the principal objectives of the Delhi Agreement. I again repeat that D.N. Barari does not represent anybody except himself. He was returned to the Bengal Legislature Assembly on the Congress ticket with the money and organisation of the Congress. He opposed the Scheduled Caste Federation candidates. Some time after his election, he betrayed the Congress and joined the Federation. When he was appointed a Minister he had ceased to be a member of the Federation too. I know that East Bengal Hindus agree with me that by antecedents, character and intellectual attainments Barari is not qualified to hold the position of a Minister as envisaged in the Delhi Agreement.

26. I recommended three names to Mr. Nurul Amin for this office. One of the persons I recommended was an MA., LL.B., Advocate, Dacca High Court. He was Minister for more than 4 years in the first FazlulHuq Ministry in Bengal. He was chairman of the Coal Mines Stowing Board, Calcutta, for about 6 years. He was the senior Vice-President of the Scheduled Caste Federation. My second nominee was a B.A., LL.B. He was a member of the Legislative Council for 7 years in the pre-reform regime. I would like to know what earthly

reasons there might be for Mr. Nurul Amin in not selecting any of these two gentlemen and appointing instead a person whose appointment as Minister I strongly objected to for very rightly considerations. Without any fear of contradiction I can say that this action of Mr. Nurul Amin in selecting Barari as a Minister in terms of the Delhi Agreement is conclusive proof that the East Bengal Govt. was neither serious nor sincere in its professions about the terms of the Delhi Agreement whose main purpose is to create such conditions as would enable the Hindus to continue to live in East Bengal with a sense of security to their life, property, honour and religion.

Government Plan To Squeeze Out Hindus

27. I would like to reiterate in this connection my firm conviction that East Bengal Govt. is still following the well-planned policy of squeezing Hindus out of the Province. in my discussion with you on more than one occasion, I gave expression to this view of mine. I must say that this policy of driving out Hindus from Pakistan has succeeded completely in West Pakistan and is nearing completion in East Pakistan too. The appointment of D.N. Barari as a Minister and the East Bengal Government's unceremonious objection to my recommendation in this regard strictly conform to name of what they call an Islamic State. Pakistan has not given the Hindus entire satisfaction and a full sense of security. They now want to get rid of the Hindu intelligentsia so that the political, economic and social life of Pakistan may not in any way be influenced by them.

Evasive Tactics To Shelve Joint Electorate

28. I have failed to understand why the question of electorate has not yet been decided. It is now three years that the minority Sub-Committee has been appointed. It sat on

three occasions. The question of having joint or separation electorate came up for consideration at a meting of the Committee held in December last when all the representatives of recognised minorities in Pakistan expressed their view in support of Joint Electorate with reservation of seats for backward minorities. We, on behalf of the Scheduled Castes, demanded joint electorate with reservation of seats for Scheduled Castes. This matter again came up for consideration at a meeting called in August last. But without any discussion whatsoever on this point, the meeting was adjourned sine die. It is not difficult to understand what the motive is behind this kind of evasive tactics in regard to such a vital matter on the part of Pakistan's rulers.

Dismal Future For Hindus

29. Coming now to the present condition and the future of Hindus in East Bengal as a result of the Delhi Agreement, I should say that the present condition is not only unsatisfactory but absolutely hopeless and that the future completely dark and dismal. Confidence of Hindus in East Bengal has not been restored in the least. The Agreement is treated as a mere scrap of paper alike by the East Bengal Government and the Muslim League. That a pretty large number of Hindus migrants, mostly Scheduled Caste cultivators are returning to East Bengal is no indication that confidence has been restored. It only indicates that their stay and rehabilitation in West Bengal, or elsewhere in the Indian Union have not been possible. The sufferings of refugee life are compelling them to go back to their homes. Besides, many of them are going back to bring movable articles and settle or dispose of immovable properties. That no serious communal disturbance has recently taken place in East Bengal is not to be attributed to the Delhi Agreement. It could not simply continue even if there were no Agreement or Pact.

30. It must be admitted that the Delhi Pact was not an end in itself. It was intended that such conditions would be created as might effectively help resolve so many disputes and conflict existing between India and Pakistan. But during this period of six months after the Agreement, no dispute or conflict has really been resolved. On the contrary, communal propaganda and anti-India propaganda by Pakistan both at home and abroad are continuing in full swing. The observance of Kashmir Day by the Muslim League all over Pakistan is an eloquent proof of communal anti-India propaganda by Pakistan. The recent speech of the Governor of Punjab (Pak) saying that Pakistan needed a strong Army for the security of Indian Muslims has betrayed the real attitude of Pakistan towards India. It will only increase the tension between the two countries.

What Is Happening In East Bengal Today

31. What is today the condition in East Bengal? About fifty lakhs of Hindus have left since the partition of the country. Apart from the East Bengal riot of last February, the reasons for such a large scale exodus of Hindus are many. The boycott by the Muslims of Hindu lawyers, medical practitioners, shop-keepers, traders and merchants has compelled Hindus to migrate to West Bengal in search of their means of livelihood. Wholesale requisition of Hindu houses even without following due process of law in many and non-payment of any rent whatsoever to the owners have compelled them to seek for Indian shelter. Payments of rent to Hindu landlords was stopped long before. Besides, the Ansars against whom I received complaints all over are a standing menace to the safety and security of Hindus. Inference in matters of education and methods adopted by the Education Authority for Islamisation frightened the teaching staff of Secondary

Schools and Colleges out of their old familiar moorings. They have left East Bengal. As a result, most of the educational institutions have been closed. I have received information that sometime ago the Educational Authority issued circular in Secondary Schools enjoining compulsory participation of teachers and students of all communities in recitation from the Holy Koran before the school work commenced. Another circular requires Headmasters of schools to name the different blocks of the premises after 12 distinguished Muslims, such as, Jinnah, Iqbal, Liaquat Ali, Nazimuddin, etc. Only very recently in an educational conference held at Dacca, the President disclosed that out of 1,500 High English Schools in East Bengal, only 500 were working. Owing to the migration of Medical Practitioners there is hardly any means of proper treatment of patients. Almost all the priests who used to worship the household deities at Hindu houses have left. Important places of worship have been abandoned. The result is that the Hindus of East Bengal have got now hardly any means to follow religious pursuits and performance of social ceremonies like marriage where the services of a priest are essential. Artisans who made images of gods and goddesses have also left. Hindu Presidents of Union Boards have been replaced by Muslims by coercive measures with the active help and connivance of the police and Circle Officers. Hindu Headmasters and Secretaries of Schools have been replaced by Muslims. The Life of the few Hindu Govt. servants has been made extremely miserable as many of them have either been superseded by junior Muslims or dismissed without sufficient or any cause. Only very recently a Hindu Public Prosecutor of Chittagong was arbitrarily removed from service as has been made clear in a statement made by Srijukta Nellie Sengupta against whom at least no change of anti-Muslim bias prejudice or malice can be leveled.

Hindus Virtually Outlawed

32. Commission of thefts and dacoities even with murder is going on as before. Thana offices seldom record half the complaints made by the Hindus. That the abduction and rape of Hindu girls have been reduced to a certain extent is due only to the fact that there is no Caste Hindu girl between the ages of 12 and 30 living in East Bengal at present. The few depressed class girls who live in rural areas with their parents are not even spared by Muslim goondas. I have received information about a number of incidents of rape of Scheduled Caste Girls by Muslims. Full payment is seldom made by Muslims buyers for the price of jute and other agricultural commodities sold by Hindus in market places. As a matter of fact, there is no operation of law, justice or fair-play in Pakistan, so far as Hindus are concerned.

Forced Conversions In West Pakistan

33. Leaving aside the question of East Pakistan, let me now refer to West Pakistan, especially Sind. The West Punjab had after partition about a lakh of Scheduled Castes people. It may be noted that a large number of them were converted to Islam. Only 4 out of a dozen Scheduled Castes girls abducted by Muslims have yet been recovered in spite of repeated petitions to the Authority. Names of those girls with names of their abductors were supplied to the government. The last reply recently given by the Officer-in-Charge of recovery of abducted girls said that "his function was to recover Hindu girls and 'Achhuts' (Scheduled Castes) were not Hindus". The condition of the small number of Hindus that are still living in Sind and Karachi, the capital of Pakistan, is simply deplorable. I have got a list of 363 Hindu temples and gurdwaras of Karachi and Sind (which is by no means an exhaustive list) which are still in possession of Muslims. Some of the temples have

been converted into cobbler's shops, slaughter houses and hotels. None of the Hindus has got back. Possession of their landed properties were taken away from them without any notice and distributed amongst refugees and local Muslims. I personally know that 200 to 300 Hindus were declared non-evacuees by the Custodian a pretty long time ago. But up till now properties have no been restored to any one of them. Even the possession of Karachi Pinjirapole[ii][2] has not been restored to the trustees, although it was declared non-evacuee property sometime ago. In Karachi I had received petitions from many unfortunate fathers and husbands of abducted Hindu girls, mostly Scheduled Castes. I drew the attention of the 2nd Provisional Government to this fact. There was little or no effect. To my extreme regret I received information that a large number of Scheduled Castes who are still living in Sind have been forcibly converted to Islam.

Pakistan 'Accursed' For Hindus

34. Now this being in brief the overall picture of Pakistan so far as the Hindus are concerned, I shall not be unjustified in stating that Hindus of Pakistan have to all intents and purposes been rendered "Stateless" in their own houses. They have no other fault than that they profess the Hindu religion. Declarations are being repeatedly made by Muslim League leaders that Pakistan is and shall be an Islamic State. Islam is being offered as the sovereign remedy for all earthly evils. In the matchless dialectics of capitalism and socialism you present the exhilarating democratic synthesis of Islamic equality and fraternity. In that grand setting of the Shariat Muslims alone are rulers while Hindus and other minorities are zimmies who are entitled to protection at price, and you know more than anybody else Mr. Prime Minister, what that price is. After anxious and prolonged struggle I have come to

the conclusion that Pakistan is no place for Hindus to live in and that their future is darkened by the ominous shadow of conversion or liquidation. The bulk of the upper class Hindus and politically conscious scheduled castes have left East Bengal. Those Hindus who will continue to stay accursed in Pakistan will, I am afraid, by gradual stages and in a planned manner be either converted to Islam or completely exterminated. It is really amazing that a man of your education, culture and experience should be an exponent of a doctrine fraught with so great a danger to humanity and subversive of all principles of equality and good sense. I may tell you and your fellow workers that Hindus will allow themselves, whatever the treat or temptation, to be treated as Zimmies in the land of their birth. Today they may, as indeed many of them have already done, abandon their hearths and homes in sorrow but in panic. Tomorrow they strive for their rightful place in the economy of life. Who knows what is in the womb of the future ? When I am convinced that my continuance in office in the Pakistan Central Government is not of any help to Hindus I should not with a clear conscience, create the false impression in the minds of the Hindus of Pakistan and peoples abroad that Hindus can live there with honour and with a sense of security in respect of their life, property and religion. This is about Hindus.

No Civil Liberty Even For Muslims

35. And what about the Muslims who are outside the charmed circle of the League rulers and their corrupt and inefficient bureaucracy? There is hardly anything called civil liberty in Pakistan. Witness for example, the fate of Khan Abdul Ghaffar Khan than whom a more devout Muslim had not walked this earth for many years and of his gallant patriotic brother Dr. Khan Sahib. A large number of erstwhile

League leaders of the Northwest and also of the Eastern belt of Pakistan are in detention without trial. Mr. Suhrawardy to whom is due in a large measure the League's triumph in Bengal is for practical purpose a Pakistani prisoner who has to move under permit and open his lips under orders. Mr. Fazlul Haq, that dearly loved grand old man of Bengal, who was the author of that now famous Lahore resolution, is ploughing his lonely furrow in the precincts of the Dacca High Court of Judicature, and the so called Islamic planning is as ruthless as it is complete. About the East Bengal Muslims general, the less said the better. They were promised of autonomous and sovereign units of the independent State. What have they got instead ? East Bengal has been transformed into a colony of the western belt of Pakistan, although it contained a population which is larger than that of all the units of Pakistan put together. It is a pale ineffective adjunct of Karachi doing the latter's bidding and carrying out its orders. East Bengal Muslims in their enthusiasm wanted bread and they have by the mysterious working of the Islamic State and the Shariat got stone instead from the arid deserts of Sind and the Punjab.

My Own Sad And Bitter Experience

36. Leaving aside the overall picture of Pakistan and the callous and cruel injustice done to others, my own personal experience is no less sad, bitter and revealing. You used your position as the Prime Minister and leader of the Parliamentary Party to ask me to issue a statement, which I did on the 8th September last. You know that I was not willing to make a statement containing untruths and half truths, which were worse that untruths. It was not possible for me to reject your request so long as I was there working as a Minister with you and under your leadership. But I can no longer afford to carry this load of false pretensions and untruth on my conscience

and I have decided to offer my resignation as your Minister, which I am hereby placing in your hands and which, I hope, you will accept without delay. You are of course at liberty to dispense with that office or dispose of it in such a manner as may suit adequately and effectively the objectives of your Islamic State.

Yours sincerely,

Sd./- J.N. Mandal
8th October, 1950

□□□